Muscle Testing for Succ

=:+:=:+:=:+:=:+:=:+:=:+:

MUSCLE TESTING

Muscle-testing exercises

applied to success topics

=:+:=:+:=:+:=:+:=:+:=:+:=:+:=:+:=:+:=:+:=:

- Hands-on experiments to unblock how we receive and manifest abundance

- Success from the cellular level on up; the TWO Games of Success each of us must play

Bruce Dickson, MSS, MA

Best Practices in Holistic Self-Healing Series

300 level material

Resources by and for self-muscle-testers

Tools That Heal Press

HealingToolbox.org

HealingToolbox.org

Simultaneously published as *Success Kinesiology, Dowsing for Success* and *Muscle Testing for Success*. All editions virtually the same except for unique covers.

Muscle Testing for Success
Muscle-testing exercises applied to success topics

ISBN-13: 978-1502870995

ISBN-10: 1502870991

CreateSpace assigned

Copyright 2013 Bruce Dickson

Other publisher inquiries welcome

.v\V/v.

To Learn More:
http://HealingToolbox.org
Bruce also recommends http://MSIA.org

Tools That Heal Press
Resources composed by and for self-healers and self-muscle-testers of all persuasions

- Best Practices in Self-Healing System Series

- Composing your own vision of self-healing

- Common terms for personal-spiritual growth

HealingToolbox.org

- Source code for self-healing

All books below available in PAPER with diagrams and charts or eBook without most images.

All written with humor and insight by a practicing Health Intuitive.

NEW in 2014: Unconscious Patterns 101, Tools for the Hero's Journey of Self-healing
Picking up where NLP metaprograms left off, expanding the topic in the context of 'God is my Partner.'

You are a Hologram Becoming Visible to Yourself - Making the invisible part of the "bigger you" visible and perceptible.

Your Habit Body, An Owner's Manual Our habits are our best friends; why then, do we make the same errors over and over again?

- **Self-Healing 101! Seven Experiments in Self-healing,** You Can Do at Home to Awaken the Inner Healer, 2nd edition

- **Meridian Metaphors,** Psychology of the Meridians and Major Organs

- "**Willingness to heal** is the pre-requisite for all healing" revised edition coming 2014

HealingToolbox.org

- ***You Have Three Selves Vol ONE***; Simply the clearest model of the whole person; Orientation
- ***You Have Three Selves; Vol TWO*** Simply the clearest model of the whole person, Find the 3S in your life & pop culture
- ***The Inner Court***: Close-up of the Habit Body
- ***The NEW Energy Anatomy***: Nine new views of human energy; No clairvoyance required.
- ***Radical Cell Wellness—Especially for women!*** Cell psychology for everyone; A coherent theory of illness and wellness
- ***The Five Puberties,*** Growing new eyes to see children afresh
- ***How We Heal; and, Why do we get sick?*** Including 35 better, more precise questions on wellness and healing, answered by a Medical Intuitive
- ***You have FIVE bodies PACME***; Spiritual Geography 101
- ***The Meaning of Illness is Now an Open Book,*** Cross-referencing illness and issues

Rudolf Steiner's Fifth Gospel in Story Form Topics include the TWO Jesus children and the active participation of the Buddha in the Christ event.

COMING Muscle Testing as a Spiritual Exercise coming 2014

HealingToolbox.org

COMING *Measuring with 'God as your Partner;'*
Scales of 1-10, math and geometry

Cover images and longer descriptions at end of this book

To Learn More:

http://HealingToolbox.org ~ **310-280-1176**

All these dedicated to John-Roger. Without you, J-R, these resources would not exist.

Bruce also recommends www.MSIA.org It helped me put myself back together again.

> The best solution is always loving

> If you get stuck, give me a call.

> v\V/v

Table of Contents

Leading Thoughts — 12

Abundance from the perspective of soul — 13

Success from the inside out — 15

Habit Body 101 — 17

Examples of habits on each level of our personality — 18

HealingToolbox.org

Our habit body is like a tensegrity sculpture   20

Education, how our firmware is usually altered   21

Our habit body is 90% to 95% of our psyche   22

Why we so easily feel overwhelmed   23

Chunking down our habit body into smaller "chunks"   24

Relationship Body 101, just an intro   24

Health Body 101, brief intro   25

To Learn More for this chapter   26

Chapter 2 ~ Success Body 101   26

Chapter 3 ~ Your Success Numbers, how to use them   29

The Seven Dimensions of Success, self-assessment tool   30

Seven dimensions of success   31

Discussion of "Success with People"   33

Chapter 4 ~ The Game of Success is not one game, it's TWO   37

OUTER Game makes your business phone ring with new clients   37

The Outer Game is your "client funnel"   37

The Outer Game is the Extraverted Game   38

Your INNER Game of Success is enjoying life and 'smiles per day'   39

When your OUTer Game is your weaker Game   40

When your INner Game is your weaker Game   41

Role models inform and remind us what being successful feels like   42

The Two Games of Success operate primarily sub- and unconsciously   43

Teaching Success as if it was only one Game   44

Athletic approach to the two games   45

Q: Why TWO games? Why can't it all be One? 47

Basic tools for your Success Toolbox   47

Chapter 5 ~ You are alive on THREE frequency levels   48

Reach out to the "bigger you" for support   49

The Frog Prince motif   51

Chapter 6 ~ The Law of Rumi applied to success   53

Our core issues peel like a cooked artichoke   54

Put the Law of Rumi to work for you   56

Chapter 7 ~ Success at cell-level-intelligence   57

Outer-facing-cell-wall reality   58

Inner-facing-cell-wall reality   59

Extraverted outer-facing cell walls are like puppies   61

Inner-facing cell walls are like cats   63

Self-assessment exercise   64

Inner Game of Success LAUGHING experiment   66

Physical organ aspect of our Success Games   70

Chapter 8 ~ What is my willingness to be profitable?   71

What's in your wallet? An Inner Wealth experiment to do at home   72

How old do you feel?   73

Is having money safe for me now?   74

Do I trust having more money now?   74

How was money lost in the past?   75

How do I feel having more money?   75

How healthy rich people feel about money   75

Chapter 9 ~ Self-testing as "Listening to your universe"   76

Client-Controlled Kinesiology, Client-controlled Testing   77

Chapter 10 ~ What is my willingness to heal?   79

Self-assessment   80

Introduction to neck-up ~ neck-down testing   80

Example of how we are split neck-up and neck down   81

HealingToolbox.org

Measure your willingness to heal on any health concern   82

How do I increase my willingness to heal?   83

Being-of-two-minds blocks willingness to heal   84

When we are of ONE mind   85

What causes us to be of two minds?   85

Chapter 11 ~ What is my willingness to receive?   86

Advanced topics   87

Chapter 12 ~ Explaining the Inner & Outer Game to Family & Clients   87

The Inner Game of Tennis 87

Chapter 13 ~ Success comes in on your most-open sensory channel   90

KAVOG and success   90

From VAKOG to KAVOG   91

How does my child within represent abundance?   93

Sensory abundance exercises   94

Our two minds have different most-open sensory channels   96

Self-assessment ~ Which sensory channel is most open in my rational mind?   98

Self-assessment ~ Which sensory channels are most open in my habit body?   99

Greater success means addressing and resolving your blocks to success   100

When professional coaching does not work   101

Intimacy as "into-me-see"   105

Greater success always feels surreal at first   108

Experiments to verify neck-up and neck-down are different for you   109

Conclusion   112

Your body is the bridge between you and Spirit   113

APPENDICES   113

Only way to change something in a mirror--is to change yourself   113

Mirror Game fairy tale   115

Inner Game Exercise: 122

Likability self-test   122

Faulty beliefs to self-assess   123

"My body tightens up..." experiment   126

"It's easy for me" self-assessments   126

Prosperity beliefs for self- assessing   127

HealingToolbox.org

Personal Power beliefs to self-assess　128

Self-Esteem beliefs you can self-test　128

Spirituality beliefs to self-assess　129

Grief/Loss beliefs you can self-test　129

Trigger beliefs to self-test　130

Negative messages you may have overheard in the womb　132

7 Success beliefs to self-assess　133

Five Personal Needs to self-assess from Wm. Glasser　134

Relationships as the source of unhappiness　136

Create your own Needs Preference Profile　136

Final words: "Always Use Love All Ways"　137

About the Author　138

Tools That Heal Press Booklist　138

Best Practices in Energy Medicine Series　139

The two best sellers:　139

Connect with the Author　174

Sessions with the author　174

Training with the Author　175

Other products　176

Reading Group Guide for Self-healing Series 176

Books outside the Best Practices Series   178

Stand-alone 99 cent eBooks tangential to Best Practices Series   178

Other CLASSICS of self-healing & Medical Intuition   179

v\V/v

Leading Thoughts

A thousand people are whacking away at the branches [lack of profitability] for every one person attacking the roots ~ Thoreau

Earth life is not not set up for our success. It's set up as opportunities to learn the lesson of how to love it all ~ Anon.

Walk no path that does not have loving on it at the beginning, on the way and at the end.

~ Healing Toolbox

v\V/v

Abundance from the perspective of soul

What does abundance look like from the perspective of our immortal-eternal soul?

It might look like this: as souls we are consciousness. Consciousness is not poor.

If we are poor here in the human expeience, we have become lousy receivers, lousy managers of what is present.

Maybe as a woman, you have guilt over getting your own needs met while others go unfed. Receiving without guilt, worthy to receive without guilt, is a wonderful topic to address, measure and self-heal on. Now you can.

The Law of Rumi says, if you wish more receptivity, address your blocks to receptivity, chip away at them to inch back into rhythms of generosity and gratitude in daily life.

This may sound boring to masculine yang-bangers; yet, is crucial to women, holistic coaches and practitioners. Indeed, redeeming the dysfunctional aspects of our Inner and Outer Game of Success is a core healing activity for consumers of holistic products and services.

The poorer a particular holistic practitioner is, the more likely the depth and balance of their two Games of Success is shallow. Find here **muscle testing** self-healing exercises to track your Success Numbers back into more patience, gradualness, kindness and rhythm.

v\V/v

This book presents something simple. However when concepts and language are new, simple things may appear more complex than they are.

Prepare for a journey unlike any other success book we know of at this time. We hope it inspires many to adopt-adapt these self-testing exercises for use with self and with clients.

This book assumes readers already have exposure to self-muscle-testing of some kind. Maybe you know:

- Kinesiology testing,

- K-testing,

- muscle testing,

- self-testing, self-muscle-testing,

- dowsing or

- inner testing of some kind

—or you are willing to learn.

Dr. Lin Morel and I made 15 videos, Muscle Testing Redesigned with 'God as your Partner: YouTube: http://www.youtube.com/watch?v=igrhezqeglg

A Muscle Testing Practice Group DVD is available. It address difficulties in testing.

Stay connected with your self and with each other,

HealingToolbox.org

Bruce Dickson, Healing Toolbox, 2014

Success from the inside out

The last time I looked, Amazon books had 123,000 books on "success;" too many to look at in one entire lifetime.

The vast number of success titles clearly suggest several things clearly:

1) People really want to learn to be more successful,

2) Very effective Tools That Heal for this purpose have yet to be developed and widely shared.

3) If an effective Tool That Heal existed to increase personal success; and was known and shared, most of 123,000 different success methods would become obsolete.

I honor earlier success methods and training and have learned from them; however, a "Looking back" article in the Appendix was finally removed as more confusing than useful.

Q: When did self-muscle-testing as a reliable method for success self-healing become viable?

A: The first very effective Tools That Heal for uncovering, addressing and clearing sub- and unconscious blocks and obstacles to personal

HealingToolbox.org

success were unlikely, perhaps impossible, before 1990.

Q: Why?

A: Three resources had to converge: self-muscle-testing, NLP and ecumenical spirituality. Sorry it took so long to write and deliver this method. If converging these three resources was easy to frame and articulate, I'm sure someone would have done it sooner. New syntheses often require a long journey to articulate what is seems obvious afterwards.

I hope if you find the Success Numbers and other exercises here effective, and share them widely.

If you get stuck, give me a call. I'm over at http://www.HealingToolbox.org

v\V/v

Habit Body 101

Dg-habits-ape-starlet

Your habit body is all your habits on all your levels, physical, imaginal, emotional, mental and mythological. You have habits on ALL these levels.

HealingToolbox.org

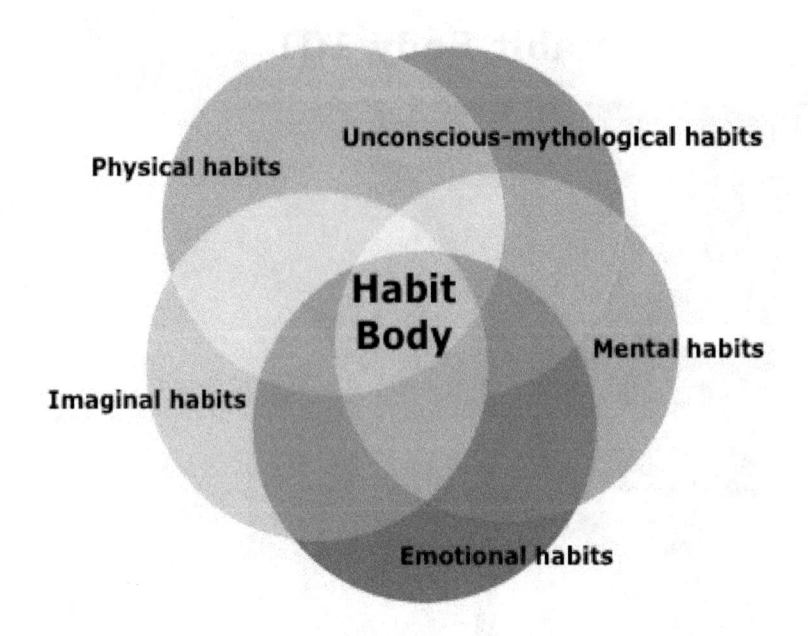

Dg-habits-color-circles

Examples of habits on each level of our personality

Physical habits: posture, breathing pattern, reflexes such as eye-blinking and peristalsis, how you walk, use a shovel, ride a bicycle, tie a knot in a necktie.

Imaginative habits: what we fantasize about and how often, patterns of day dreaming, habits of expectation, habits of liking and disliking about people, places and things. Habits of ambition and revenge.

Emotional habits: over- and under-participation with people and commitments. Habits of over-giving, under-giving and withholding

Mental habits: self-talk, self-judgments good or bad, cherished beliefs good or bad; "things my grandmother used to tell me;" finally, faulty and obsolete beliefs and allegiances.

Mythological habits: favorite memories; favorite pet fears, favorite role models, favorite boogeymen.

Our habit body is most clearly conceived of as a 3D hologram. Picture-imagine the millions of connections you must have between various sets of habits, for each role you play in your life.

Main article on the scheme of PACME is in *You have FIVE bodies; Spiritual Geography 101.*

Our habit body is like a tensegrity sculpture

Dg-tensegrity

Ever see a tensegrity sculpture? It's wooden sticks held in relationship with no stick directly touching any other stick. Rubber bands stretched between the sticks and the tension on these strings holds everything in place.

This reflects how our neurons are organized, all close, but not touching.

Q: WHY are our neurons arranged this way?

A: The answer is so obvious, so big we miss it. If every neuron was connected with every other neuron from the start, no possibility for learning would exist. Learning in human nature is making choices and strengthening connections between neurons by repeated use.

Our immune system does something specific when ideas and behaviors are repeated. Thoughts, impulses, and behaviors repeated causes the brain to mylenate (protect, establish) those pathways so that impulse can travel more easily that pathway in the future.

It's common to contrast this with the neurology of a baby horse, a colt. The baby colt is born, immediately gets up, starts nursing and behaving horse-like. Her actions are driven by "firmware" usually called "instincts."

When you were born, what happened? You probably don't recall. In fact, it probably took you several years before you could rub two brain cells together and know that was you, doing your own thinking.

The openness of human neurology, the absence of massive instinctual "firmware" means individuals can build up very unique sets of habits. Humans were entrusted with creating their own "firmware."

If you need an example of how flexibly human beings can be programmed, just look around Earth at the variety of cultures.

Education is how our firmware is usually altered

K-12 education is where our habit body and firmware receive most of our programming, firmware and what we can humorously call "instincts."

If after high school and after college, you wish to make significant changes to your own firmware, your habit body, most graduate schools are not going to be that useful, if your goal is personal-spiritual growth. Grad school in 2014 exists primarily to train technocrats for high paying jobs.

To alter your success firmware, in your Inner and Outer Games of Success, in your sub- and unconscious, a topic not yet in any grad program, you can begin doing your own research and your own experiments, at home.

Self-testing is that workable, reliable experimental method to assess, access and explore clearing blocks and obstacles in your Success Body.

Our habit body is 90% to 95% of our psyche

Dg-see-saw

If we imagine a children's playground and the piece of playground equipment called a see-saw or teeter-toter, it may surprise you to hear your Habit Body is balanced by only 5% to 10% of another capacity in human psyches.

The 5% to 10% of our psyche capable of balancing the other 90% to 95% is our ability to make waking, conscious, deliberate choices and decisions.

Why we so easily feel overwhelmed

It's easy to feel overwhelmed in our day because our habit body is vast compared to our immortal-eternal soul aspect, the "choice" part of us. If you ever feel overwhelmed with too many decisions, if you ever feel tired as a decision maker, this is not an illusion. Our need for rest and down-time is real.

Chunking down our habit body into smaller "chunks"

Chunking down is perhaps the premiere NLP strategy of all for dealing with our sub- and unconscious. Chunking down the huge expanse of our psyche governed primarily by habit supports our understanding of what we are up against as wakeful, conscious Deciders and Choosers.

So it can be advantageous to chunk down our Habit Body into smaller subsets of habits to look at.

If we learn to think more strategically about our habit body and segment it by category, we enable language as a tool for managing the invisible parts of our own psyche. Part of this is to make and use categories. Your Success Body is one category of habits in your Habit Body. Having names and languages reduces overwhelm managing our Habit Body.

Screening one subset of your habit body is much easier than screening the entire huge, 3D hologram of your Habit Body.

Relationship Body 101, just an intro

Imagine just the habits you have around relationships. This one subset of habits will stiff be huge but *less huge* than all your habits. That's chunking down.

Could we call this your Relationship Habit Body? We sure could. As long as we remain in the domain of one person, sure we can.

Your *Relationship Body* is all of your habits pertaining to your activity in relationships, physically, imaginally, emotionally, mentally and mythologically (PACME).

Your Relationship Habit Body would be all your habits, good and bad, socially appropriate behaviors and socially inappropriate behaviors, memories, etc. PACME.

My Relationship Habit Body will naturally be somewhat different from yours.

HealingToolbox.org

Health Body 101, brief intro

How about all your habits, PACME, around physical health and wellness? Could we call them your *Wellness Habit Body* or *Health Habit Body*? As long as we remain in the domain of one person, we sure can.

Doing so may support some readers to address their habits pertaining to to diet-nutrition, exercise, lifestyle and sleep.

Get the idea? Your Success Body is all your habits pertaining to your success and failure in manifesting your goals and projects in the 3D world.

To Learn More for this chapter

Find full discussion of the PACME+Soul model in, "You have FIVE bodies PACME, Spiritual Geography 101" http://www.healingtoolbox.org/k2-stub/item/209-you-have-five-bodies-pacme-spiritual-geography-101

Find full discussion of habit body here: *Your Habit Body; An Owner's Manual*
https://www.createspace.com/3416647

and here:

You Are a Hologram Becoming Visible to Your Self
https://www.createspace.com/4106814

v\V/v

HealingToolbox.org

Chapter 2

Success Body 101

In the same way, anyone can experiment chunking down all your habits around material success into a Success Body.

Q: Where is it?

A: It's a sub-set of your larger Habit Body. Your entire Habit Body is sub- and unconscious; therefore your Success Body is located there too. "Success habit Body" might be more clear for some readers. You decide which terms works best for you.

Q: Why can't I see my Success Body?

A: For the same reason you cannot see your Habit Body. Your sub- and unconscious is invisible to animal eyesight.

Q: If I can't see my Success Body, how do I access, explore it and improve it?

A: You can access, explore and improve your Success Body the same way people access, explore and improve ANY part of their Habit Body, with methods-techniques-arts on the Energy Medicine Skill Ladder. The first modern reliable experimental method for sub- and unconscious issues was self-muscle-testing converged with NLP and ecumenical spirituality, after 1990.

HealingToolbox.org

Which methods you choose depends on how much natural talent you have. The middle-level method is self-muscle-testing but meridian tapping and Gestalt two chairs work are easier for many and also work fine. The Skill Ladder is here: http://www.healingtoolbox.org/k2-stub/item/333-skill-ladder-of-holistic-healing-methods-techniques-arts

Q: Why restrict and narrow my focus to look at only one subset of habits in my habit body?

A: In high school, did each of your teachers teach all subjects in every class: English, Spanish, Geography, Math, Spots, and History all together? Or did you chunk down knowledge into sections and segment them as distinct classes by the day, by equipment available, by applicability and so on? Divide and conquer. Overwhelm is the biggest problem in approaching our sub- and unconscious.

Before 1990, virtually holistic and conventional practitioners were both overwhelmed with challenges inherent in accessing invisible sub- and unconscious material. 50 to 100 different talk therapy methods competed head-to-head in the 20th century as the "best way" to access and navigate invisible sub- and unconscious material.

After 1990 self-muscle-testing converged with NLP and ecumenical spirituality, enabled enuf precision to access invisibles, if only primarily in the domain of one person.

For purposes of self-healing, experiments only have to work for you so "the domain of one person" is not a limitation.

Learning to be more materially successful has something fundamental in common with learning to tie your own shoelaces at five years old. Both are habits. When a habit becomes automatic or semi-automatic, we call that "success."

Tying your shoelaces is a physical routine, hand-eye coordination. Material-social success involves many more habits, levels and <shudder> other people, a much wider range of habits to coordinate. That's all.

Q: It still sounds too complex to understand.

A: Understanding is NOT called for here. EXPERIMENTS are what is called for. If you will experiment, you will learn how your Success Body works. The only wrong ways to experiment is not to try at all; and, try it egotistically, without any form of spiritual self-protection from Soul and Above.

The Success Numbers routine compacts all these ideas into simple paper and pencil self-assessments anyone can do, any time. If you get stuck, give me a call.

v\V/v

Chapter 3

Your Success Numbers, how to use them

If opportunity does not knock--build a door ~ Milton Berle (found in Debbie Bermont's *Outrageous Business Growth* book)

I hope by the end of this book, you will have ten, twenty, fifty sets of your own Success Numbers, "snapshots" of the health of your Success Body. If you do ten experiments you will begin to see patterns. By experiment #50, you are likely to see several positive progressions. That's all you have to do, all I do myself: keep chipping away at the blocks and obstacles to positive flow, on all levels with 'God as my Partner.'

May as well get busy. The Seven Dimensions to test are below.

Measure your Success Body from each of the seven angles on a scale of 1-10, ten being optimal for you and only you, today.

Why wait? Get your first set of Success Numbers.

Q: Wait, I don't know how to muscle test!

A: No problem. Start by guessing. Only wrong way to do this is never begin at all. "Guessing" has a technical name, a "Likert Scale;" learn about it at Wikipedia for support using guessing as your method.

HealingToolbox.org

Q: What if I do it wrong?

A: Not possible. You can always meet the minimum requirement for success in experimenting: what I just tried did not work; this gives me an idea for what to try new next time.

Make your goal this: to learn one or more new things each time you measure your numbers.

If you keep measuring, over time, you will learn how your system works. Only you can learn how to test better for your needs.

The Seven Dimensions of Success, self-assessment tool

 After a couple years of research and experiment; then, numerous "guinea pigs," I developed a Success Profile self-assessment paper and pencil instrument. It took this long to compose a comprehensive hologram of our Success Body in English; and then, field test its stability. By 2011 it was working well.

How to use it?
1) Self-assess with the Success Profile,

2) It identifies the weakest of your seven dimensions of success today, for you,

3) Address, clear and strengthen your weakest link with any Energy Medicine method comfortable for you to experiment with now.

HealingToolbox.org

I encourage people to learn this and teach others.

Seven dimensions of success

Our Habit Body is a 3D hologram. This means any sub-set of our habit Body must also be a 3D hologram, and this is logically so.

it appears SEVEN aspects of success can encompass the length, breadth and depth of our Success Body.

These seven have been stable over time. If you find an eighth or nine dimension to incorporate, please share with me for testing.

Verbatim duplication encouraged as long as credit is given to HealingToolbox.org

1) Willingness to have money and own material things ___/10

2) Willingness to engage with, be interested in, be successful with, and enjoy people ___/10

3) Willingness to support yourself, be self-supporting in the material 3D world ___/10

4) Willingness to assist other people with their goals and dreams ___/10

5) Willingness to partner with your own child within in your 3D success ___/10

6) Willingness to chunk down, into bite-sized pieces, both your goals and challenges, so your

inner child can process; and take, consistent, daily baby steps forward ____/10

7) Willingness to partner with your own Divinity in your success, to invite God to be your Partner in Your success ____/10

The Success Profile Instrument points to seven facets, chunks, dimensions of your Success Body, each a facet of your Habit Body, required for manifesting material-social success.

If you measure your Success Profile tomorrow, your weakest link may have shifted; that's good. That's called "progress." Do another experiment, find your new weakest link and strengthen it.

Discussion on #2 "Success with People"

This is liking people, willingness to reach out to people in person and by phone, to "reach out and touch someone;" also, to be seen by people, to be visible.

To be successful in biz, especially in the social media age, means you have to love people and find ways you enjoy engaging with them.

The prerequisite for loving people is loving yourself, your own feeling mind, your inner child, your Little Artist and your own body.

If you don't love your self, then "know you > like you > trust you > buy from you" becomes disturbed.

Persons with low self-love benefit most from inner child work and Little Artist work of all kinds

If this is a weak measure for you, ask yourself, "Was I ever successful with people?" You might have been successful...

Socially in junior high

Socially in high school

Socially in college

Currently have a supportive spouse and family of some kind?

Success with peers and colleagues?

Success as a leader in volunteer organizations

If none of these apply to you, and your goal is to become a successful practitioner, spend time with friends and mentors who can assist you by pointing out where you need to Lighten Up or Go Deeper in your own self-acceptance.

Q: What else? I'm still stuck. What else can I use to move my lowest number?

A: I'm glad you asked!

With SEVEN dimensions of success—instead of one-whole-cake called "success," It's much easier to measure, test, check how the child within is oriented, where it willingness—and where it has less. This gives you a more straight shot at raising your lowest numbers.

None of these measurements have anything to do with you from the neck-up. Forget it. This is for your non-dominant mind, your inner child; who is from your neck down, more precisely, from our diaphragm muscle down, from your breathing muscle down, your habit body.

Measuring either from your neck down or from your diaphragm muscle down will get you a valid Success Profile but you please stick with one way or the other; don't mix them!

Q: How do I write down my responses?

A: I've tried various journals. A simple form works best for me. Currently I use sheets of printer paper cut up into quarter-sheets. Each time I test, I generate one of these hand-drawn forms. I used to print them and have printed them for class use with students. What works for you?

Q: I don't understand these Seven Dimensions. What are they and where do they come from?

A: That's what the rest of the book is for. Eventually all you need is the self-evaluation exercise, so first things first.

Q: Over time why do my numbers change, go up and down?

A: Because you are changing. The changing numbers reflect changes in you.

Q: Once I raise a number, does it stay high?

A: No, it can go down before it goes up again.

Q: Why?

A: Two answers to this. One is as you clear blocks and obstacles in your habit body, you as a whole expand; your field expands. As your consciousness loosens and relaxes, it expands. So lower numbers reflect how old numbers are now a smaller percent of a larger whole.

Second way to understand why-how numbers can go down: Rubik's Cube.

As you make one of the six faces of the cube more color-coherent, the other five faces become less color-coherent. To get two or more faces of a Rubik's Cube color-coherent, is a long journey, of many steps because all six faces are inter-dependent; the color-coherency of each individual face is in part a function of the coherency of the other five faces.

The human psyche is a 3D hologram with exactly analogous process.

The above two metaphors support us working with this instead of against our habit body.

HealingToolbox.org

Changing number results means you KEEP GOING; you're not done yet. Get support! Your best hope is to keep going forward to becoming more coherent, more integrated and more aligned.

Q: I thought "success" was one thing, a single thing.

A: This was a MAJOR problem with earlier ways at looking at and measuring success.

As NLP says, many nouns betray us. Many words we use as nouns are really complex processes. NLP's definition of a 'legal noun' is something you can carry in a wheelbarrow. Ever try to carry "success" in a wheelbarrow? "Success" is a process, a long list of interconnected habits, a subset of habits in our habit body.

v\V/v

Chapter 4

The Game of Success is not one game, it's TWO

In our Habit Body we are always playing TWO games, an Inner Game and and Outer Game.

These two games are very conspicuous and obvious in our Success Body.

OUTER Game makes your business phone ring with new clients

The Outer Game is anything you do to attract and keep customers, your systems; including, employees and assistants.

How you reach out to new clients and make your phone ring client calls, is many habits put together.

What you do to make the phone ring with existing and new clients; and less of everything else, is your Outer Game of Business.

The Outer Game is your "client funnel"

Whatever you do to attract and keep customers, engaging existing and new clients in the progression of:

> know about you,
>
> like you,
>
> trust you,
>
> want to support you, so they...
>
> buy from you.

The job of your client funnels is to engage existing and new prospects with the benefits of you and your product/service.

Your Outer Game includes your contact list, your friends, your software, your social media, anything you do to connect with new and existing friends, your volunteers, assistants and employees.

The Outer Game is the Extraverted Game

- how you show up in the world, how visible you are,

- how favorably your biography and public profile is perceived by others,

- how inviting, timely and attractively packaged your services and product line is,

- how clearly you address your ideal client and new people.

In a phrase: your public platform, appearance and presentation.

Without the Outer Game, the market, your audience and Abundance can't find you!

If winning at the *Outer* Game of Business is your first and foremost goal—this may not be your book. For that goal, I recommend asking Mr. Google about:

marketing freebies

promotion free

marketing CDs free

HealingToolbox.org

Your INNER Game of Success is enjoying life and 'smiles per day'

How you enjoy the fruits of your labors, how you feel about what you have accomplished in your work, how nourished you feel by your lifestyle and schedule—that's another Game entirely, isn't it?

How many times today did someone touch you in a way making you smile with enjoyment? Can you savor how delicious it feels to shift from needs-not-met to needs-fulfilled? Inner Game is:

- Nourishing yourself in feeling safe, trusting your self, trusting others, trusting the world, trusting God,

- Satisfying yourself nutritionally, sexually, emotionally, spiritually,

- Connecting with your immune-system-self, comfortable asking to have the needs of your Child Within met, keeping clear the highest good of all concerned,

- Relaxing, taking it easy on yourself, replenishing, recuperating,

- Appreciating what you have and how your biz is bringing you your lessons about both the physical and the spiritual worlds,

- Gratitude for what you have right now,

- Delicious anticipation of more benefits and pleasantries on their way towards you now.

HealingToolbox.org

The above goodies come from aligning your rational mind with your inner child. This is the foundation of your Inner Game.

Recognizing material success requires playing TWO Games, an Inner Game of Success and Outer Game of Success; and, these two games have to be roughly in balance, can be a major "Aha!" in your growth as an entrepreneur of any kind.

The more holistic, green, spiritual your biz is, the greater the need for a balance between the Inner and Outer Games.

When your OUTer Game is your weaker Game

This is the easier Game to strengthen. Everything you can do to grow your business OUTWARDLY is already online, visible and highly organized.

Strengthening your outer game of business can always be accomplished by spending more dollars strategically, tactically and wisely.

When your INner Game is your weaker Game

If you are struggling to be profitable, or in a tizzy after trying many Outer Game tactics, look to your Inner Game. Outer Game problems more often than not begin with Inner Game disturbances.

Inner Game disturbances are always more personal, uniquely personal.

Strengthening your Inner Game of Business can not always be bought, even by one-on-one coaching.

Strengthening your Inner Game of Business requires reframing, re-thinking what needs to change in your life, habits and behaviors. What's not working? What is working? How can you do more of that? These are matters of personal-spiritual growing, of maturing-up, becoming more Coherent, Integrated and Aligned (CIA) so you have more internal magnetism to attract more clients and ideal clients.

Naturally, you can self-test these variables. I do this inviting God to be my Partner; goes better, I find.

One of the most impactful things, possible to do, to grow your biz, is, to recognize you play two games, an Inner Game and your Outer Game of Business; assess the strength of each; and then, strengthen your weaker Game.

The difference between balancing your Two Games of Success is often the difference between a sustainable and profitable business; and, a part time hobby.

   Failure asks us to look deeper in both of TWO directions. Success Numbers self-assessment narrows down your weak area quickly.

HealingToolbox.org

Role models inform and remind us what being successful *feels* like

If success is elusive, chance are good your unconscious reference points for success, PACME, are weak. Role models is how our unconscious likes to learn.
You may even have memories of your own earlier success. Were you ever successful with people? You might have been successful...
with peers and colleagues in an earlier job?
as a leader in volunteer organizations?
in junior high?
in high school?
in college?
If you have memories of being successful with people in the past please exercise these memories in all five sense channels, kinesthetic, auditory, visual, smell and taste. Make the images BIG. Man readers will know this is a tactic made popular by Tony Robbins. I think it's in *The Power Within You,* certainly in other books and audios. All Tony's 1980s audio packages are now on YouTube for free so enjoy.
Persons with low self-love, benefit most from inner child work and Little Artist work of all kinds.

    If you don't love your self, then
  know you > like you > trust you > buy from you works less well.

If your goal is to become a successful practitioner, spend time with friends and mentors who can assist you by pointing out where you need to Lighten Up or Go Deeper in your own self-acceptance.

HealingToolbox.org

The Two Games of Success operate primarily sub- and unconsciously

Failure asks us to deeper in both of TWO directions.

Q: "Yah but I need to control everything"

A: Because conscious-waking self is only aware from our neck-up; and, our immune-system-self is aware both sub- and unconsciously, two-thirds of our Success Games activity is outside the view of Waking Self.

Brain wave frequency divisions make this clear:

Conscious-waking self making deliberate choices: beta brainwaves only

Sub- and unconscious activity (everything else): alpha, theta and delta

This is why control of outer things is such a frustrating game to play. We can only control consciously a small fraction of our own psyche, let alone others and the world.

Teaching Success as if it was only one Game

To exaggerate a bit, earlier success literature, beginning in the 1930s with Norman Vincent Peale, tended to approach success primarily as one game, the outer game, as if only one Game existed. Their point was: get yourself motivated and organized to play the Outer Game better.

HealingToolbox.org

Q: Why this one-sided approach?

A: Two reasons. Prior to NLP and muscle-testing in the 1990s, psych language was more primitive. No reliable experimental method, except for dowsing existed. Dowsing remained pretty obscure, known and practiced by only a few and those few were outside the professions of psychology, counseling and psychotherapy.

Second, economics. It's much easier to sell tangible than invisibles. The Outer Game is primarily visible. The Inner Game is primarily In-visible. If you selling success, it's much easier to sell products and biz services than it is to sell inner competency, inner maturity, internal coherence, internal integration and inner alignment.

Before all the success trainings of the 1980s, these issues were considered counseling and psychotherapy issues, inner stuff.

Q: Did teaching primarily the Outer Game work for many people?

A: Enuf to be profitable for some speakers. Augmenting Outer Game did work for anyone weaker in their Outer Game than in their Inner Game. At some points in our life we are weaker in one Game than the other Game.

A primary focus on improving your Outer Game did not help people who were weaker on their Inner Game.

Athletic approach to the two games

Like any athlete, ALL self-employed persons improve their game--whatever it is--by strengthening their weakest muscle or tendon first. In our case that would be, strengthen the weaker half of your Game of Success first.

If the extraverted outer Game of Success is stronger for you now-- strengthen the Inner Game.

If the introverted inner Game of Success is stronger for you now-- strengthen the Outer Game.

Q: What if I can't tell which is stronger, which is weaker?

A: We need each other to heal. Other people can often see our own out-of-balance pattern easier than you can. Ask your friends which Game of Success you are stronger in. They'll tell you.

We need each other to heal for a second reason. I highly encourage healers and coaches to work on each other for rejuvenation and so you do not get stale. Get all the assistance you can to become profitable.

One thing masterful people do is *not* take their failures so personally. They take success, and the lack of it, as helpful feedback, even if it's negative feedback. Failure tells them what NOT to do. This kind of self-transparency and vulnerability is visible from time to time in the most successful folks, Tony Robbins for example.

HealingToolbox.org

This gives us a paradox. We have to minimize personal reactivity about our own failures; at the same time, we have to take action to improve things.

Soon we will MEASURE your two games and put numbers on them.

Awareness in and of itself can be healing. Learning which Game we are stronger in, which Game we are weaker in, begins a healing process.

Q: Why TWO games? Why can't it all be One?

A: Because the soul in the human experience fundamentally experiences both an INNER and an OUTER reality. You have to play BOTH GAMES even if our culture is skewed and distorted 90% towards only the one Outer Game.

Q: How do I know when I'm IN balance between my Inner and Outer Games?

A: You have balance between taking care of your own needs; versus, taking care of others and external needs. You will arrange things so more and more, you can give from your overflow, from your joy, from your generosity and from your gratitude.

Basic tools for your Success Toolbox

Need more Tools That Heal to work the numbers? Let's acquire two conceptual tools to make doing experiments easier.

.v\V/v.

Chapter 5

You are alive on THREE frequency levels

Most blocks and obstacles to our success are going to be sub- and unconscious. This implies a map. Let's make sure we all understand this map. A handy "map" exists to navigate into new, unfamiliar areas of our psyche:

Highest frequency	Words
Middle frequency	Feelings
Lowest frequency	Needs met and unmet

Dg-words-feelings-needs

We can be conflicted and split in one or more of these.

These line up neatly with other ideas you already know:

Words   Conscious self, rational mind

Feelings   Subconscious mind, your child within, immune system self

Needs   Unconscious mind, cell-level-intelligence

Words are primarily useful only for the top one-third of our psyche, from our neck up. We process our OUTER experience primarily from the NECK-UP, where we can match our experience with words.

Raise your hand if you use language and self-talk to think about your life. I thought so. Most of us use a lot of words spoken and in self-talk.

Feelings are definitely more INNER than words. How we feel about our outer life, our environment and how we feel about what we think, comprises much of our inner experience.

Needs are definitely most inner of all. "Needs" means am I getting enuf air, water, food, shelter? Needs are very basic, survival needs. Not wants, preferences, goals or dreams.

Reach out to the "bigger you" for support

Q: This sounds like 'inner child work.' I don't care about her. I want to reach the "bigger me."

HealingToolbox.org

A: Wonderful! Your child within IS the first level of the expanded "bigger you," your psyche beyond your "little me" self.

"Island Man" (Island Woman) has to first make friends with your own child within. Then the rest of the "bigger you" opens up.

As your child within (neck down) feels safe and trusts conscious-waking mind (neck-up), connection with the high self comes automatically. The "bigger you" spiritual seekers are so keen to find can only be found by going down in frequency first. This is by angelic design, not arbitrary, not an accident, not a mistake.

Outer success is always in part a function of, a reflection of, how successful our inner cooperation and inner teamwork is. Our conscious self, from the neck up, has to first partner with our child within, our immune system, from the neck down.

The Frog Prince motif

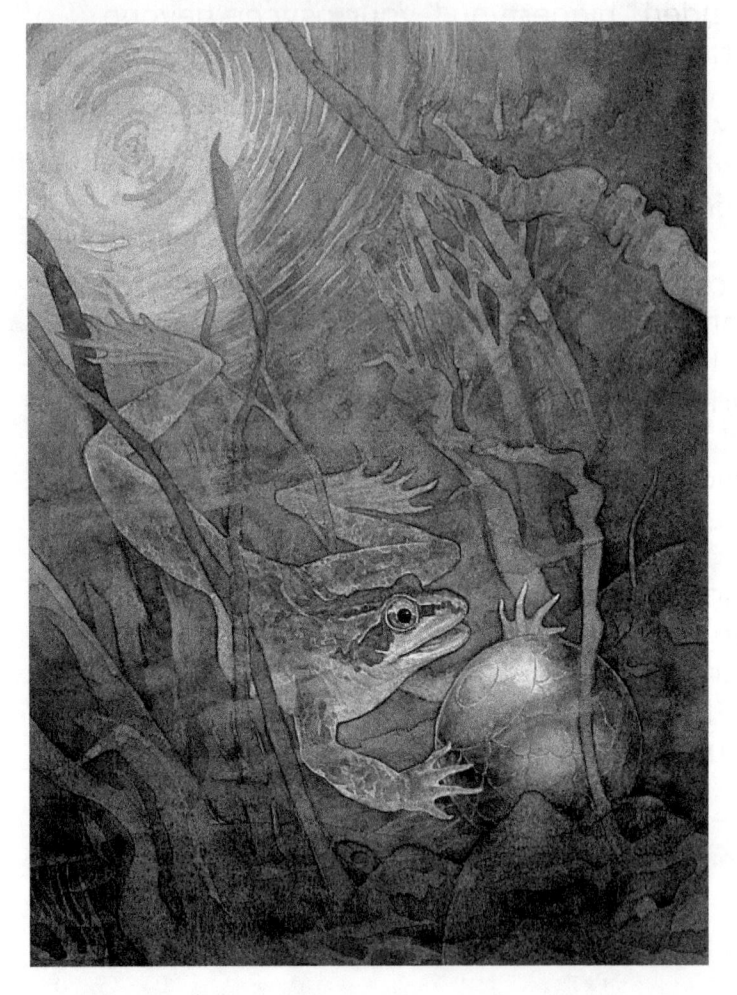

Dg-frog-prince

This motif has artistic expression in the fairy tale of the Frog Prince. Consider the Princess at the beginning of the tale: prejudiced, vain, superficial— an Island Woman.

She clearly is challenged to lower her standards; more precisely to lower her reactivity and automatic disliking enuf so she can kiss the frog, her own child within.

Her act of acknowledgement, implying kindness and affection, awakens a capable, handsome prince (male polarity) who then partners with the Princess towards greater wholeness and happiness.

"Beauty and the Beast" is a longer, more articulated version of "Frog Prince." In this case, the Frog has the upper hand; Beast is the more powerful figure.

Same pattern tho, the woman has to abandon her fear, intolerance, and prejudices to find, accept and honor the unlimited, magical ability in her own lower self.

The slow way to do this is talk therapy. The Frog Prince fairy tale does not say, "talk." The Princess throws the frog against a stone wall. The fairy tale says "experiment" and "risk."

Of course if you have no other Tools That Heal in your Healing Toolbox, use talk therapy. It is slowest because talk so often cycles round and round only from the neck up, yadda-yadda-yadda.

Every method on the Energy Medicine Skill Ladder supports connection between conscious-waking self and immune-system-self. The middle-transitional skill on the Ladder is self-muscle-testing, including dowsing, the most applicable to all other EM methods. If you experiment with 'God as Your Partner' (GIMP), you'll be fine.

Q: What else works to connect with my child within?

A: Gestalt Transformational Chairwork is another way. Constellation-Psychodrama group process is a very social form of the two-chair process. Grace is a third way.

Q: Good. I'll take Grace.

A: Wonderful! Grace is available for about 10% of our disturbances. The other 90% require your conscious participation, attention and experiment. The Law of Rumi will not be mocked.

.v\V/v.

Chapter 6

The Law of Rumi applied to success

If you say, "I want to be healthy," or, "I want more Love," or, "I want more of this good thing in my life;" then, I think of what the poet Rumi said in the 1200s (updated):

You can't go after more of a positive quality directly.

What you CAN do is go after your own blocks and obstacles to your desired positive quality. Blocks and obstacles you can go after directly.

I believe this is what John-Roger implies when he said, "you have to go after spirituality indirectly."

It also connects with the idea, "The fastest way to change something, is to take personal responsibility for it." A tip of the hat to University of Santa Monica Spiritual Psychology program for this.

The Law of Rumi is the strongest general therapeutic direction I know of.

This puts "what not to do" in the positive: what you CAN do. We can always go after our blocks and obstacles to health-success-joy-love. If we perceive, name or locate a block or obstacle, awareness alone can be healing.

Another strong therapeutic direction might be: Our blocks to our OUTER Game of Success will primarily be from the neck-up, things we know we can or should do, we have not followed thru on 100% yet.

Our blocks to our Inner Game of Success will primarily be from the neck-down, in our sub- and unconscious.

Greater outer success must result as we acknowledge, address and ultimately resolve our stumbling blocks to success.

Our core issues peel like a cooked artichoke

Close-up with any one person's obstacles to success and abundance you see how individual and unique e are. Our psyche is not designed to make books easy to write about it. Our psyche IS designed so, those who wish to, can access your own issues by your self or with a mentor. We need each other to heal.

One of he best and most rewarding uses of time here on Earth is coming together, to assist each other, to learn new skills, to connect, and learn from each other.

Our individual healing process has two thrusts:

- Being of service, sharing our gifts and talents with others,

- Working on our own unresolved issues with a Healing Buddy, mentor, etc.

Our core issues flake off like peeling a cooked artichoke. Keep peeling and work your way towards the heart of the matter; that's the really good part.

Peel away, leaf by leaf:

3) Top leaves (conscious issues) ~ You know what needs to change here or any friend can tell you.

2) Middle leaves (subconscious issues) ~ Dialog with your inner child. Anyone who can talk with your inner child can assist you to explore and redirect habits here.

3) Artichoke heart Core issues (unconscious) ~ Waking-conscious self is mostly blind and deaf to our own core issues.

Complicating matters, our unconscious has little to no language compared to our rational mind. Our unconscious issues cannot speak; or if they can, they talk like Tarzan or the Incredible Hulk, "Me hurt; me no feel good." You have to ask for assistance to reach these, to get enuf language and imagery going for the purposes of clearing. About 10% of these issues can be cleared thru Grace and do not have to be worked thru more consciously. Since 90% of our issues do have to be worked thru towards some resolution, this is why we need each other to heal.

Put the Law of Rumi to work for you

- Perceive what is working, what is not,

- acknowledge what is not working,

- point to and locate habits in need of your attention,

- address,

- identify,

- accept,

- have compassion for,

- forgive,

- resolve and

- renegotiate old habits and behaviors into updated habits and behaviors that work better for us.

Q: HOW do I do this?

A: Well, there's this Success Numbers routine you use with self-muscle-testing. Want to give it a try?

You did already? Fantastic. Below are more tools to work it.

If you don't know where your weakest link is, take your own inventory find out where you are "split." Find your weakest link? Find it. Work with it. That's what I do. When I'm in denial about this stuff—my healing takes longer.

Ultimately your Success Body rests on how balanced your cells are playing the Inner and Outer Games of Success. Let's learn how our cells think about "success."

.v\V/v.

Chapter 7

Success at cell-level-intelligence

Our Inner Game of Success seems to have its deepest roots in our psyche at our cell level, in how one cell perceives life.

If you've listened to Bruce Lipton (*Biology of Belief*), you'll recall each cell has TWO cell walls, inner- and outer-facing, not just one boundary layer.

Bruce Lipton 101 says in part the brain of our cells is not the DNA; rather, its is the cell walls; the inner-facing and the outer-facing cell walls, taken together, BOTH cell walls, that's the cell brain.

Success is perceived as one thing by our outer-facing cell wall.

Success is perceived as very differently by our inner-facing cell wall.

The deepest logical level where the Two Games are played appears to be here in the contrast between how our cells experience life in our two cell walls.

   Your outer-facing-cell-wall is the foundation of your OUTER Game of Success.

Your inner-facing-cell-wall is the foundation of your INNER Game of Success.

The deepest logical level where the Two Games are played appears to be our cellular level.

Outer-facing-cell-wall reality

Your outer-facing-cell-wall surveys the external environment, looking for nutrients and messages coming at it. Think extraversion. Our outer-facing cell wall is the deepest level of our psyche playing an OUTER Game of Success.

Inner-facing-cell-wall reality

Our inner-facing-cell-wall surveys the inner environment of one cell, sensitive to harmony, balance, too-dry, too-hot, too acid too alkaline, oxygen levels, etc. Think introversion. Our inner-facing cell wall is the deepest level of our psyche playing an INNER Game of Success.

Your outer-facing-cell-walls are the foundation of your OUTER Game of Success.

Your inner-facing-cell-walls are the foundation of your INNER Game of Success.

Q: In every cell?

A: I don't know. We have different categories of cells, some reproduce and some do not. Blood cells look a whole lot different from muscle cells. This is a technical question beyond my expertise. What I'm good at and pointing to is the PATTERN.

If you have the means to research this in more detail, will you please inform me of what you find? Probably a team using both muscle testing and clairvoyance could run such questions to ground in a week.

Like many aspects of energy, the dynamic works across cell category differences. This is more about life in earthly form, not about specific cells per se.

Any visualization of your cells with both an outer- and inner-facing cell wall will work. That's all the cell biology I needed to get started.

HealingToolbox.org

Q: Where can I get a review of the thrust of Bruce Lipton's topics?

A: Dr. Mercola wrote a summary here, Epigenetic vs. Determinism:
http://articles.mercola.com/sites/articles/archive/2012/04/11/epigenetic-vs-determinism.aspx

Q: Where can I see Bruce's charts, diagrams and animations?

A: His full course of cell biology and its significance for our psyche and habit body is on many hours of 2010 and earlier lectures on YouTube. I recommend the first three chapters of *Biology of Belief* if you have never read it. Still very timely.

I like the idea if I correct things at my cell level, results will "cascade" up into everywhere else in my life, according to my willingness to heal.

For every ten people clipping at the branches of evil, you're lucky to find one hacking at the root ~ Thoreau

For every 123,000 books on Amazon on "success," you're lucky to find a few people working at the unconscious and cellular level of success.

Extraverted outer-facing cell walls are like puppies

Dg-puppy

Outer-facing cell walls are like puppies. They want to sense, sense, sense. Their enthusiasm for the external environment is unlimited.

Healing Toolbox speculates our outer-facing cell walls are the beginnings and origins of what we call extraversion and extraverts.

Second, outer-facing cell walls first want to trust; they want to trust the environment, that it will be at least somewhat predictable, that today will be not too different from yesterday.

If the cell wall believes the surrounding environment is toxic or hostile, it will pull in its receptor sites and make itself minimally available to external threats (and nutrients).

HealingToolbox.org

Assuming for the moment, the coast is clear and it's a "sunny day," outer-facing cell walls look out to the external liquid environment, alert to snatching nutrients and matching available nutrients with their receptor sites.

Each cell wall has various receptor sites. Some look like antennas, sticking out on its periphery. These receptors accept nutrients, like amino acids and enzymes, whose chemical "key" shape fits the chemical "lock" shape on the cell's receptor site.

Successful cells allow appropriate nutrients, fitting existing criteria, to pass the cell wall so they can enter the interior of the cell.

Our outer-facing cell wall also lets out, releases, CO_2 and other spent products and waste materials, no longer useful for optimal internal function.

Don't get bogged down in the biology. Healthy outer-facing cell walls are like healthy, happy puppies.

Inner-facing cell walls are like cats

Dg-cat-contentment

Success for inner-facing-cell-walls is contentment, perceptions of internal well-being and needs met.

Am I toxic or safe? Am I coherent? Integrated? How closely am I able to reproduce according to my own DNA instructions? The inner life of our cells measures itself against its own version of Divinity, most probably DNA and its experience of reproducing if it is a cell that does split and reproduce.

Success inside our cells might be phrased as, "I am safe. I am ready, willing, able and open to getting all my needs met. I am enjoying and savoring all my needs being met now."

Isn't that similar to how we divide and perceive our outer career goals and work, our Two Games of Success?

HealingToolbox.org

By the way, I just learned, or just understood, how beliefs are what modify our receptivity in our cell receptor sites. This is the epi-genetics aspect of Bruce Lipton's ideas. Cell-receptors were first discovered on the outside of cells, facing out, facing and tasting the environment. However, if I understand correctly, some receptor cells face inside to taste the intra-cellular environment. Faulty beliefs (mostly about worthiness?) can limit receptivity and diminish choices possible to make from our environment.

Readers wishing more material on cell-level Best Practices are invited to check out *Radical Cell Wellness—Especially for Women* https://www.createspace.com/3576820

Self-assessment exercise #Two

With the above sketch of success at cell-level-intelligence, let's come back to conscious-waking self. This is as good a time as any to experimentally measure your two Games of Success right now.

Each reader can make two measures, one for each Game.

Since TWO Games exist, you wish to track two numbers, see how they compare to each other, track their progress over time.

a) On a scale of 1-10, ten being optimal for me today, my Outer Game of Success is at ____/10.

b) On a scale of 1-10, ten being optimal for me today, my Inner Game of Success is at ___/10.

If you don't use self-muscle-testing yet, you can simply use a subjective scale of 1-10. This will feel like guessing. That's fine.

Again, use self-testing if you can do it; use guessing if you have to. If you can test more inwardly, Inner Testing, by all means, do that.

Q: Okay. One of my two Games has a lower number. Now what?

A: There are clearly three cases:

1) You can do nothing. That's fine.

2) You can be curious about WHY one Game yielded a lower number. You can open up your own Healing Toolbox, take out whatever tools you have, and explore what's keeping your number low. That's fine.

3) If you get stuck, see your friendly neighborhood Healing Coach, someone you trust and can learn from. That's fine.

Q: I'm going to work on this myself but I need more Tools!

A: The first most useful tool for everyone seems to be Slow-Motion Forgiveness™. You can see it at http://www.HealingToolbox.org. See other tools I like further below.

Q: What if I need help with BOTH games?

A: Take hope. This is a workbook-manual of experiments for your success

v\V/v

Inner Game of Success LAUGHING experiment

We each have four frequency zones, head to foot, in our body. We know these as four frequencies of laughing, hee-hee, ha-ha, heh-heh, and ho-ho. These are arranged vertically.

Dg-laughter zones diagram
These vertical zones arise from how our etheric body is apportioned between the four characteristic qualities of ether. Our four laughter zones can be used as a measuring tool for where our Inner Game of Success is strong and weak.

Two main articles on the four laughters are here: http://www.healingtoolbox.org/articles/best-practices-in-energy-medicine/490-laughter-yoga-four-vertical-frequency-divisions-in-our-etheric-body-head-to-toe-easier-than-chakras

And here:

http://www.healingtoolbox.org/articles/best-practices-in-energy-medicine/498-laughter-as-energy-medicine-measure-how-successful-you-are-by-laughing

The four laughs of Laughter Yoga are:

Hee-hee, also Tee-hee-hee!

This laugh comes from the head, from the neck up. It is related to Beta brainwave frequencies. Waldorf educators will know hee-hee is the characteristic laugh of the young child as young children are proportionately much more "head beings" than adults.

Ha-ha!

Ha-ha, also Ah-ha! comes from our chest and heart region. This is approximately Alpha and some Theta brainwave frequencies. The more free and loose our diaphragm muscle is, the bigger our ha-ha laugh is; so, I suspect ha-ha is well-connected with diaphragm muscle, our breathing muscle. The lung meridian is paired with the diaphragm muscle in Touch for Health.

Hey-hey, or heh-heh

This is our weakest laugh; heh-heh is often only a chuckle. It comes from the "chuckle region above our belly button and below our breathing muscle, the diaphragm muscle. Theta brainwaves dominate here.

HealingToolbox.org

Ho-ho-ho!

The Santa Claus laugh, comes from our belly button down to our feet. Delta brainwave frequencies dominate here.

The relative strength of each of these laughs reflects our openness, relaxation and flexibility in each of these regions.

Therefore, the four laughs can be used to focus our attention and learn where we are most free and most blocked, top to bottom, in our body and psyche.

Laugh hee-hee out loud, focus on the neck up. Then say, "Money and clients come to me easily." Does this feel strong to say? Can you muscle test? Do you test strong or weak on this statement after laughing this way?

Laugh ha-ha-ha! out loud a few times, focus on your heart and lungs. Then say, "Money and clients come to me easily." Does this feel strong to say? Can you muscle test? Do you test strong or weak on this statement after laughing this way?

Laugh ho-ho-ho! out loud, focus on your belly button. Then say, "Money and clients come to me easily." Does this feel strong to say? Can you muscle test? Do you test strong or weak on this statement after laughing this way?

Where you test strong, your success mechanism is working. Where you test weak, unresolved obstacles are present to your abundance, in the level of those brainwave frequencies.

What to do when a laugh tests weak

Please don't feel like the Lone Ranger on this. We all have invisible "monkey wrenches in the works" to acknowledge, find and remove. You'll find sorting out and clearing the issues blocking your abundance much easier to do with a Healing Buddy or a Healing Coach. "Where two or more are gathered..." is not a fairy tale it's real and more true everyday as Earth's frequency rises.

Whatever tool in your Healing Toolbox moves or shifts the issue is beneficial. There is no one way to do this because everyone heals uniquely.

Other phrases to test with laughing

People and clients love my work.

It's easy for me to engage in selling conversations with people.

My appointment book fills up easily each week with clients I love spending time with

What affirmations can you come up with?

If you get stuck, please give me a call.

Physical organ aspect of our Success Games

Lots of accessible psychology exists here for those looking for it. Our internal organs participate in and reflect how we are doing on our two Games.

Our organs "take their orders" from the strength and relative balance of our YANG and *yin*. Hence, our bilateral internal organs reflect our Yang-yin balance most clearly.

For most people our digestive organs will be of greatest interest.

On our right side our liver and gallbladder take their cues from how healthy our YANG polarity is.

On our *left* side, our stomach, pancreas, spleen take their cues from how healthy our *yin* polarity is.

Find full discussion of the Game of YANG we play on the right side of our body and the Game of *yin* we play on our left side in *NEW Energy Anatomy* here https://www.createspace.com/3540877

Find full discussion of *Meridian Metaphors, Psychology of the meridians and major organs* here: https://www.createspace.com/3416642

v\V/v

Chapter 9

What is my willingness to be profitable?

Self-assessment exercise #3

"Profitability" here means—at a minimum--profit to take care of your basic needs plus at least a little left over. At a maximum, "profitability" means profit enuf to give money away to support people and causes you believe in.

"Profitability" here does NOT mean "greed" or some abstract number of millions of dollars divorced from who you are and your willingness to serve yourself and others.

One way to ask this is:

My willingness to be profitable in my business today, on a scale of ten is _____/10.

A second way is:

What is my willingness to be profitable in my business today?

A third way to ask this is:

On a scale of 1-100, 100 being optimal for me today, how willing as I to be profitable in my business?

Yes, you can ask this globally, combining neck-up and neck-down.

Yes, you can ask it separately for each of neck-up and neck-down.

What numbers did you come up with?

Did you guess or did you self-test? Both are good places to start.

What's in your wallet? An Inner Wealth experiment to do at home

I heard an Access Consciousness practitioner share an exercise. He asked his subconscious an open-ended question: how much money it felt comfortable having in his wallet.

You can ask your subconscious how much money it likes to have, an exercise with your child within.

He or she will probably feel comfortable with a different amount of money than you from the neck-up.

What's in your wallet? Inner Family version
Self-assessment exercise #4

Checking with the inner child is good. A more precise and effective way to do this is checking all four quadrants of the child within, an idea from Babinetics.com. The easiest close-up view of the Inner Child is a system of four quad-

HealingToolbox.org

rants. Each quadrant is semi-autonomous and requires asking individually using muscle testing of any method.

The Inner Game of success for me includes checking aspects of my psyche for blocks and obstacles to success—on their terms. If I have inner parts willing to have less money, or no money, in its wallet, compared to me, the conscious self, I want to know!

When I check my quadrants, I quickly learn my weakest quadrant, the one most in need of my love, attention and education.

Sure enuf, having done this on myself and a few clients, the pattern seems to be if an individual has issues with money-poverty, one or more of the quadrants in the head imagines itself as having little or no money, an empty wallet.

Analysis question: How old do you feel?

I ask my poorest part, "When you think about having little or no money—how old do you feel?'

This very often surfaces an age in my present biography where I have unresolved feelings and felt unsupported. Slow-motion Forgiveness is a good tool to go forward; as well, any method on the Skill Ladder of Energy Medicine is likely to work for you.

Analysis question: Is having money safe for me now?

In our unconscious, very simple considerations pertain. The first is:

- Is having more money safe for me now?

I like to measure this on a scale of 1-10, ten being completely for me today.

HealingToolbox.org

I work out any kinks uncovered.

Analysis question: Do I trust having more money now?

A second cell-level-intelligence consideration is:

Do I trust having more money? If I make it, will it stay around; or, do I just spend it immediately?

To simplify: Do I trust if I make more money, I can keep and save it?

I like to measure this on a scale of 1-10, ten being optimal for me today.

If money is either unsafe to have; or, keeping more money feel shaky, I like to check if the disturbing issue is in the categories of:

   Self, Other people I know, the World, God-Divinity

Analysis questions: How was money lost in the past?

Especially if money is not trustable, I like to ask my subconscious part:

- Did you lose your money?
- Did you give it away?
- Was it taken from you?
- Other trauma with money?

For me, once my unresolved disturbances are more clear, I like to ask how much money each quadrant would like to have in their wallet/purse.

How do I feel having more money?

A goal for the Inner Game of Success is feeling comfortable with the feeling of having more money. Make sure this is a positive feeling. If having money is sub- or unconsciously a bad feeling for you—guess what?

How healthy rich people feel about money

Healthy rich people feel: "I do not have to spend my money immediately; I can save money for a rainy day;" or, "for my child's education, etc."

Healthy rich persons feel they have enuf money they do not need to spend it all on necessities.

They can look in their purse/wallet and feel, "I have money left over I do not have to spend now."

How much is in my own wallet now? Personally, I like $200.00 in my wallet today that I do not have to spend for necessities.

Beyond this outline work with individuals is—individual because each person heals somewhat uniquely.

If you get stuck, give me a call.

v\V/v

HealingToolbox.org

Chapter 10

Self-testing as "Listening to your universe"

Are you paying attention to the questions Life is asking you? Are you hearing what Your Universe is telling you?

If you are struggling economically, simply taking in and working with what your Universe is telling you can be a life saver, a life raft for your biz.

Q: What do mean "listen"?

A: "Listen" in this book means "acknowledge and pay attention to what's out of balance so you can correct it." This is a big part of using the Earthly experience to our advantage.

"Listening" as used here connotes kindness, patience, compassion and gentleness for your child within as the two of you work together.

Self-muscle-testing enables measuring many aspects of where we are out of balance. Self-muscle-testing can be used both for identifying disturbances; and, for resolving them, if you so choose.

If you are struggling economically, self-muscle-testing can be a life saver, a life raft to learn WHERE you are out of balance; and, what to do about it. If you get stuck, find a Healing Coach, someone who has solved the problems you are now facing.

HealingToolbox.org

Client-Controlled Kinesiology, Client-controlled Testing

Peace Theological Seminary (PTS.org), in the Masters and Doctorate programs, teaches what I call Client-Controlled Kinesiology Testing. This is a "mouthful" that means: each individual student forms her own questions and makes all her own interpretations of her own test results. In other words, the person asking the questions also decides what the test results mean. You answer your own questions, with your immune system as your Partner.

A second person present, who pushes down on the student's arm if needed, is ONLY there to press down on an arm. Only the testee gauges muscle responses. Even if the pusher-helper interprets muscle results differently from the client—they say nothing. The pusher-helper neither forms the question nor evaluates any responses. The pusher-helper is only there to support and serve. No rescuing, no helping, no interpreting. Just be the Light for the client to find their own way. The two roles are reversed and then you have the pleasure of not hearing their interpretations of what your muscles are doing, either.

You can do a LOT for yourself if you can self-test; or, work with a friend to be your pusher-helper—then—switch roles.

This hard and fast firewall between tester-testee and the pusher-helper solves the problem of expert testers, such as chiropractors, doing 50 tests in 60 seconds and then telling you what is wrong with you and what you need. They may be accurate. However the process is not empowering clients. Client-Controlled Kinesiology Testing is clearly designed so you learn from your own testing in a feedback loop.

This "hands off" approach also aligns with another Law of Self-Healing: Each Person Heals Uniquely.

PTS also teaches asking for the Highest Good and Greatest Loving to be present before you test. You'll try that, won't you?

Q: So when success books stop working for me, I have to look down into my feelings and needs and learn what is unresolved?

A: You got it!

Q: HOW do I address the bottom two-thirds of my psyche?

A: With the exercises in this book, or better ones, if you can find them. This book offers the most recent solutions and exercises for this purpose. This is the book I wish I had had, when I was in my 20s.

Q: Where do I start?

A: Find 15 videos on Client-Controlled Testing (CCT) on YouTube by me and Dr. Lin Morel HERE: https://www.youtube.com/channel/UCV_fRTd-Cz5J85uz5WXhx0g/videos?view=0

A Muscle Testing Practice Group DVD is available. It address difficulties in testing.

HealingToolbox.org

v\V/v

Chapter 11

What is my willingness to heal?

What do infants have? They have Willingness

When we are born, what do we exhibit in our behavior? What is happy-new-baby-behavior primarily? It is not "will;" it is not "willfulness."

Newborns certainly do not have "will power."

Healthy babies have willingness. They demonstrate willingness.

This is what we are trying to get back to as adults on any path of personal-spiritual growing: healthy willingness, expanding this.

Self-assessment #5

This is the "global" version. Measure your "willingness to heal" globally first, for everything in your life you wish to heal.

The next exercise will be about testing individual issues-concerns.

Please DO THIS NOW. Get a second person to assist you if you need to do a two-person Client-Controlled self-test.

HealingToolbox.org

My willingness to heal, on a scale of ten is ____/10.

Introduction to neck-up ~ neck-down testing

We have several natural divisions in our etheric body invisible in physical-material anatomy. These are most fun to explore with the four kinds of laughter. They are spelled out in *NEW Energy Anatomy*.

In simplest terms, faster tempos are higher in our body; lower tempos are lower in our body, towards our feet.

The educated an individual is, the more able they are to think and live in their faster tempo higher frequencies.

This only becomes a problem when we live ONLY in our higher frequencies, higher in our body and lose track of the wholeness of our psyche.

Living too much in the head has been likened to "living in an ivory tower." If we transpose this to a body-based metaphor, one of the easiest ways to think about this is as a split between us from the neck-up and us from the neck-down.

HealingToolbox.org

Example of how we are split neck-up and neck down

Everyone wants healing; just ask them; they say, "Of course I want to be healthy, healed of my concerns!"

This tells us their response from the neck up, from their rational-waking-conscious mind.

For self-healing, your job is to check from the neck DOWN, to check willingness in the inner child. Why? To learn if both of your two lower selves are working together or not. Remember, the job of our two lowest selves is to learn to work together as teammates and partners.

Measure your willingness to heal on any health concern

Self-assessment #Five ~ What's my willingness to heal specific concern: _____?

Measuring your willingness to heal neck-up and neck-down is simplicity itself.

1) Pick, identify, write down one single health concern.

2) Measure your willingness to heal this concern from your neck up ____/10.

3) Measure your willingness to heal on this concern from your neck down ____/10.

HealingToolbox.org

Please DO THIS NOW. Get a second person to assist you if you need assistance.

From the neck up represents the interest and desire in your rational mind for healing your target.

Measuring from the neck down tells you how much inner cooperation you have on this from your silent partner, your immune system.

If the two numbers are low or both far apart, it tells you, you are not lined up for healing.

Measuring both neck-up~neck-down disperses many inaccurate inner pictures of who is doing what and how things happen in our psyche and body.

Measuring twice, once for neck-up again for neck-down above and below the neck yields a more accurate picture of where you are.

Q: Can I measure my willingness to heal on a single concern in each of the four laughter zones?

A: Absolutely. This is a Best Practice in Self Healing. Find your weakest link and apply your loving attention there.

Earthly life was designed to make the conscious self curious. Too bad we became know-it-alls prideful of what we know, dismissive of things outside our ken. That was NOT the Plan.

If differences between your neck-up and neck-down measures makes you curious--good. There is much to learn.

HealingToolbox.org

How do I increase my willingness to heal?

This is so simple we forget. Ask. Asking is a soul action. Attention and intention are soul actions.

This can be is where affirmations, the main additive process in self-healing, are useful. Positive affirmations can support when willingness to heal is low. Repeating what you want more of, and tapping around your belly button can wake up your enteric nervous system to get on board with what you are affirming.

However, most of our unresolved issues are cleared thru subtraction. Forgiveness is the main subtractive soul action. Slow-Motion Forgiveness (SM) is one version of this http://www.healingtoolbox.org/tools-that-heal/64-slow-motion-forgiveness

The Law of Rumi and Forgiveness applied to blocks and obstacles you uncover are the way out and up many times.

If you get stuck, give me a call.

Being-of-two-minds blocks willingness to heal

'Inner cooperation' means being of one mind, not two. John-Roger once said inner cooperation is the biggest karma on the planet.

In Birth Plan numerology, the number two (2) symbolizes inner cooperation. Inner cooperation is the conscious self--the yak yak mind--being on the same page as the immune system, both looking the same direction and seeing the same goal.

One of these will be your dominant mind, technically your dominant nervous system. The other will be your non-dominant mind, your non-dominant nervous system.

WARNING ~ this is NOT the same as sympathetic and parasympathetic nervous systems. This is cerebral nervous system and gut brain. Find more discussion in *You Have Three Selves, Vol. 1: Orientation* and in the forthcoming book on *Enteric~Cerebral*.

For optimal self-healing, both nervous systems need to work as a team. They need to be attending to the same concern and both come to acceptance, compassion, understanding, forgiveness, and so on.

When we are of ONE mind

Being of single mind, one focus on one dream, one goal, one passion increases our energetic strength. This not usually done thru willpower. It's usually done thru harmony, balance and rhythmic application of baby steps, like waves on the shore wearing down even the hardest rocks.

When your rational mind and non-dominant mind are both looking the same direction and seeing the same goal (J-R), they are working together, cooperating, collaborating teamed up. You have two minds and this is a good thing; like, having two hands.

What causes us to be of two minds?

Bertrand Babinet (Babinetics.com) suggests excess reactivity is what primarily causes us to be split. He suggests unmonitored excess reactivity is the main stumbling block in personal-spiritual growing. I agree. The top-dog may be looking one way—but the underdog may have its eye elsewhere. Perhaps this is the meaning behind the physical symptom called "lazy eye."

The other big thing splitting us up is risking new creative enterprises and projects without securing adequate support for our own needs first. In a phrase: going out on a limb. I call this the Indiana Jones error. It's discussed soon below.

.v\V/v.

Chapter 12

What is my willingness to receive?

Self-assessment #Six ~ Willingness to receive?

Please DO THIS NOW. Get a second person to assist you if you need to do a two-person Client-Controlled self-test.

    My willingness to heal, on a scale of ten is ____/10.

Measuring your willingness to receive neck-up and neck-down, is simplicity itself.

1) Pick, identify, write down one single person-place-thing you wish to receive more of.

2) Measure your willingness to receive this from your neck up ___/10.

3) Measure your willingness to receive this from your neck down ___/10.

Please DO THIS NOW. Get a second person to assist you if you need assistance.

.v\V/v.

Advanced topics

Chapter 13

Explaining the Inner & Outer Game to Family & Clients

The Inner Game of Tennis

Some readers will know the original Inner Game idea comes from the classic book, the *Inner Game of Tennis*. Long before *Chicken Soup for the Soul*, *Inner Game* became a books series and a small "industry."

A somewhat forgotten topic in the 2000's, *The Inner Game of Tennis* can easily be retrieved simply by scanning the book reviews at Amazon.com, here one somewhat revised for clarity:

A phenomenon when first published in 1972, the *Inner Game of Tennis* was a real revelation. Instead of serving up a new way to hit tennis balls, it was not promoting an external technique. As Gallwey wrote, it concentrated on how, "Every game is composed of two parts, an outer game and an inner game."

The former is played against opponents. Each coach has their own contradictory advice. The Inner Game is played not against anyone, but within the mind of the player. Its principal obstacles are self-doubt and anxiety.

Gallwey's revolutionary thinking, built on a foundation of Zen thinking and humanistic psychology, was a primer on how to get out of your own way to let your best game emerge. It was sports psychology before the two words were pressed against each other and codified into an accepted discipline. Billie Jean King, a world-famous tennis pro of yore, called the original book her tennis bible.

The new edition of this remarkable work refines Gallwey's theories on concentration, gamesmanship, breaking bad habits, learning to trust yourself on the court, and awareness. "No matter what a person's complaint when he has a lesson with me, I have found the most beneficial first step is to encourage him to see and feel what he is doing--

HealingToolbox.org

that is, to increase his awareness of all that is present uniquely for him as a player."

Aspects of psychobabble and mysticism can be found here, sure, but Gallwey instructs as much by anecdote as anything else. Time has proven him a worthy guru. What seemed radical in the early '70s is now accepted and canon: a positive, non-judgmental mental approach is every bit as important as a good backhand. *The Inner Game of Tennis* still does much to keep that idea in play – Reviewed by Jeff Silverman

Another review:

The "inner game" of tennis is the game taking place in the mind of the player. It is played against barriers such as nervousness and self-doubt. The book looks at the idea of "Self 1" and "Self 2." Self 1 is the "teller" and Self 2 the physical doer, the performer.

Self 1 likes to tell Self 2 how to hit the ball and play the game. We have all caught ourselves talking to ourselves and heard others talking to themselves during a game. If you ask someone who they are talking to, they will usually say, "I'm talking to myself." This, of course, implies that there are 2 "selves", "I" and "myself"- and so is born the idea of Self 1 and Self 2.

[Thus how the idea of conscious self and basic self, the key concept of the Three Selves, pertains in sports psychology.] To achieve peak performance, the key is to resolve any lack of harmony between your two selves. It is usually the contrary thinking of Self 1, the "inner critic," which interferes with the natural abilities and learning of Self 2.

Quieting an active inner critic can come from releasing self-judgments, letting Self 2 do the hitting, recognizing and trusting the natural learning process...

The inner obstacles Gallwey is talking about are fear of failure, resistance to change, procrastination, stagnation, doubt, and boredom. Gallwey shows you how to tap into your natural potential for learning, performance, and enjoyment so any task, no matter how long you've been doing it, or how little new you think can be learned from it, can become a fresh opportunity to sharpen skills, increase pleasure, and heighten awareness.

When purpose, passion and business converge in a person and reflect in coherent outer, physical habits and behaviors, such a person's practice takes off and flies.

\v\V/v/

Chapter 14

Success comes in on your most-open sensory channel;

KAVOG and success

A major way to begin partnering with your child within is to pay attention to its most-open sensory channel. Only one or at most two of these will be most-open in an individual:

One or at most two of these will be common ground between conscious-waking self and your immune-system-self.

This common ground is where your child within will most often share with you its perceptions.

You have five choices:

Kinesthetic ~ feelings, impressions, body sensations, touch, warmth

Auditory ~ sounds, voices music, self-talk, recorded messages from parents

Visual ~ inner colors, clairvoyance, inner visions, day dreaming, NOT movies or TV or video games (that's something else).

Olfactory, smell, flowers, roses, essential oils

Taste

Gustatory, taste, bitter, sweet, etc.

First you have to identify your inner child's most-open sensory channel.

From VAKOG to KAVOG

KAVOG began with VAKOG, in NLP, the topic of sensory channels. VAKOG was first published in *The Structure of Magic Volume 2* (1975) by Richard Bandler and John Grinder.

NLP arranged the five sense modes from the perspective of the conscious-waking self, looking from the top down. Visual (eyesight, reading, meaning) is clearly the most valuable sense channel of the waking self.

However, from the perspective of our immune-system-self, FEELING is clearly the most-used and most-valued sense. So each of our two lower selves values the five senses differently.

If we arrange them in order of how our inner child makes meaning, we start with FEELING: do I feel safe? Do I feel trusting? Then Hearing (Auditory), then, Visual, and lastly Smell and Taste. Your pattern can vary 10% or more from this, that's fine.

NLP teaches each person's habit body has some of these sensory channels open more than other channels. We call these preferences. They are based on experiences of safety, familiarity, and cultural permission about how the world comes into us, how we take in the world.

HealingToolbox.org

Our habit body makes use of KAVOG sense percepts to:

- Search for meaning and pleasure in the environment.

- Record memories for later retrieval.

Building on the theories of General Semantics from the 1930s and 1950s, which in turn echoed ancient Hindu philosophy, Bandler & Grinder described how each of us represent, sort and organize memory and experience uniquely using these sensory channels. Naturally the more open channels you have, the richer your experience of the world is for you.

NLP makes the crucial point that meaning, in our habit body, is composed of collections of sensory percepts.

Meaning trumps KVAOG. KAVOG leads to meaning. Once meaning is established and resolved, the representations tend to fade.

Q: Can this be used unethically?

A: Yes. Stage hypnotists "reprogram" just these levels to make people do ridiculous things. Don't do that. Manipulation, even in jest, is very likely to come back to you. Manipulating is showing off and little learning occurs.

HealingToolbox.org

How does my child within represent abundance?

How do you prefer to experience abundance? Some like the feel of a wallet thick with hundred dollar bills, or the feel of silk and cashmere, or time spent relaxing at a spa. All you who prefer abundance kinesthetically, please raise your hands. Today I found a three year old girl for whom abundance was measured in "tastes good."

Some people like to hear they did a good job from the boss. They like the sound of money clinking in their pocket. They like to tell people how much they made and how fast they made it. Raise your hand if this is you.

Some people like to see themselves driving a fast car; or, visualize their bank account numbers going up even higher and faster. Raise your hand if this is you.

Seeing dollars circulating in, around and thru your auric field works well if you are highly visual.

What is it you want to have so badly you can smell and taste it?

Do you have a taste for success? Raise your hand if this is you.

Can you smell where the money is? Many successful people can smell money, smell opportunity. Raise your hand if this is you.

HealingToolbox.org

Each of us has a relationship with success modified by our most-open sensory channels.

Want to explore your preferences? Here's a free VAK preference test:
http://www.businessballs.com/vaklearningstylestest.htm

A good NLP book for self-healers is *Core Transformation* by Connierae Andreas. This NLP book is closest to what many muscle-testing self-healers moving energy are doing. It's a hidden gem as are most of the books by Real people Press.

Sensory abundance exercises

Does money smell good to you or bad to you?

If abundance in some form smells bad to you, you are telling your unconscious not to be like that, to avoid that.

On the other hand, what if abundance is the smell of wonderful multi-dimensional flowers...!

Quiz: Identify which sensory channel success is on for each of these

How do you prefer to experience abundance? The human pattern is to have one of our sensory channels most-open to success. Identify which sensory channel each of the following images points to. Which one feels most open in you?

HealingToolbox.org

- Feel in your pocket a wallet thick with hundred dollar bills...

- The fragrance of expensive perfume...

- Sound of coins clinking in your pocket... Sound of gold coins clinking...

- See yourself driving in a fast, expensive car...

- Spend time relaxing in the Jacuzzi at a spa with a friend...

- Hanging an expensive piece of framed art on your wall...

- Seeing dollars circulating in the air around your body...

- Hear from your boss you did a good job...

- The quality of silk or cashmere on your skin...

- Big numbers in your bank account...

- When you are hungry for success, what food do you picture...

So which sensory channel does success come in most strongly for you?

No one reading this book is interested in faking success or masking failure with a pretense of success—HOWEVER--if you like the idea of "acting as if," assuming success, or earlier, ruder formulation, "Fake it till ya make it," all of these have to have one or more KAVOG sensory images. Without such imagery, how can you include and engage your inner child?

Success also has to do with allowing people closer into your own life. You can't be successful all by yourself; it takes people! Many of you will know the two dangers here, allowing people in too close; or, being too isolated. Which side of balance do you tend to err on?

So each of us has a relationship with success somewhat based on different sense modalities. How we prefer to experience success in our senses differs. The patterns here are well known in the topic of VAKOG in NLP.

Our two minds have different most-open sensory channels

Complicating inner cooperation, our conscious self has one preferred channel of communication and our habit body often has a different most-open sensory channel.

NLP practitioners report; and close observation by anyone confirms, the basic self and conscious self do not share the same representational system. The conscious self prefers making meaning with the visual sense and the habit body prefers making sense of the world thru the auditory sense. That's one common variation. Most commonly in the West, the visual channel is most open from the neck up and the auditory or kinesthetic channel is most open from the neck down.

This goes a long way to explaining why people are so often "of two minds." It also suggests the normal obstacles people encounter in attempting to communicate with their inner child.

There are two ways to look at this mismatch of preferences. Either cooperation between our two minds is more problematic; or, the difference in point of view permits us two points of view on the same experience so we can easily triangulate from our experience. All the more reason to ask for and test for a second opinion on things as "two heads are better than one." If each self has a different map of the same experience, they "see" it differently. In other words, you have two hands—this is a good thing!

It's no secret more creative thinkers enjoy multiple points of view and use multiple mapping systems. We call this flexibility.

How to recognize unresolved disturbances in the sub- and unconscious

1) Become aware something is "off."

2) Spend a minute locating where the off feeling is in your body.

3) Explore KAVOG representations of the feeling and see what emerges.

4) Ask for Light, Love and Angels to release the negativity off these impressions, redeem these impressions from the negative choices we allowed, promoted or created.

HealingToolbox.org

5) Watch how the issue resolves itself into more positive meaning and integrates with the rest of you.

Reader results may vary. If you can write a better way to explain this, let me know. Feel free to contact me for improving your ability to self-heal.

Your rational mind and non-dominant mind often prefer different ways to experience success. Here's a way to learn who prefers what:

Self-assessment #7 ~ Which sensory channel is most open in my rational mind?

My visual sensory channel is open ___/10.

My auditory sensory channel is open ___/10.

My kinesthetic sensory channel is open ___/10.

My olfactory sensory channel is open ___/10.

My gustatory sensory channel is open ___/10.

My rational mind's preferred sensory channel is: _____.

End of Measure #7

Self-assessment #8 ~ Which sensory channels are most open in my habit body?

My visual sensory channel is open ___/10.

My auditory sensory channel is open ___/10.

My kinesthetic sensory channel is open ___/10.

My olfactory sensory channel is open ___/10.

My gustatory sensory channel is open ___/10.

My habit body's preferred sensory channel is: _____.

End of Measure #8

The more sensory channels we have open to success, the more likely we are to find it and recognize it. The more sensory channels we have open, the more...

- alert we are to what works in our behaviors,

- alert we are to customer cues,

- communication we can have with our inner child,

- communication we can have with the inner child of clients.

Conversely, the fewer sensory channels open in a person, the less "human" and approachable that person is perceived by others.

How do my two minds prefer to experience success?

Q: So if my two minds prefer to experience abundance, riches and prosperity differently...?

HealingToolbox.org

A: Given the above, you can speculate on how each of your two minds prefers to experience success; in other words, thru which senses it is most open and expectant for success.

My one or two most open sensory channels for success are _____.

Greater success means addressing and resolving your blocks to success

"Success" is not monolithic, is not one thing; it's a process. As William Glasser and NLP will tell you; you're better off using the word "successing" because you can't carry success in a wheelbarrow. Both NLP and Glasser suggest changing any noun we wish to get know better into a verb: "successing." To get to success, we must practice "successing."

The Inner and Outer Games of Success make this very clear:

Successing the Outer Game means doing everything you do to build a client funnel

Successing the Inner Game means:

- acknowledging where we are not lined up inwardly,

- willingness to accept, tolerate, and address our misalignments without judging,

- willingness to be a good parent to our inner child as she learns how to "success" better,

- willingness to communicate with our misaligned parts often,

- learning adequate and sufficient new language to talk about my two minds,

- acquiring and practicing with Tools That Heal to leverage movement and change,

- for optimal results, do all this within the context of Light, Love and Angels,

- if you get stuck, give your self-healing buddy, your mentor, or SOMEBODY a call for a second opinion!

.v\V/v.

When professional coaching does not work

My Co-Chair at the Holistic Chamber quoted me a statistic: 5% of new business succeed. Of those 5% that succeed, 95% of them used some form of biz coaching or mentoring relationship.

A good biz mentor cheerleads you to take beneficial outer actions; and, face inner issues that need to be faced. Much of this is breaking out of old habit patterns, comfort zones and faulty beliefs. A good coach assists you to connect the dots between your outer business ailments and your unresolved inner conflicts.

Even so, coaches and clients sometimes come into conflict. Many of you will know coaching relationships sometimes end when the coach says, "To be profitable, you have to do something new in your Outer Game of Success, we'll call it X." For instance, "to get more clients, you will have to market first and foremost to your existing client base, the people who have already bought from you. Keep up these relationships."

The client says, "Okay, I'll do X to add to or upgrade my Outer Game by this date." But the client fails to do X by the date. Neither coach nor client can fathom what the problem is.

When both coach and client agree behavior X needs to change and the client is still unable to do X, this means the Inner Game needs re-examining. The Outer Game has little relevance to these situations When client can not X that both coach and client agree needs doing, this simply points to an underlying deeper issue, usually one neither knows much about.

If the coach is very good, he/she can lead stuck clients to uncover what deeper inner values are in conflict, what's disturbed "under the waters."

What I find is behavior X will change easily or on its own if I can arrange things so the client releases their inner barriers and attachment to old ways of doing things.

What else saps our strength as practitioners?

These are all things you can test for to see if you are in-process with them in your habit body.

- Does this or that choice-person-project create an upward or downward spiral inside me? A feeling of heaviness or a feeling of lightness?

- Am I plugged into something that is not uplifting to me?

- Am I tolerating distractions or creating scatter?

- Do I need to change something Physical: poor location, lack of $, materials...?

- Do I need to change something Imaginal: low self esteem, negative self-talk...?

- Do I need to change something Emotional: unresolved personal issues, life chaos, co-dependence...?

- Do I need to change something Mental: faulty beliefs? Treat with Psych-K.

- Do I need to change something Unconscious or Mythological: my vision, my self-concept, how I view my biography, disturbed memories from past lives?

Like you, know you, trust you, buy from you

The old marketing idea of sales and marketing is this sequence. The more people who participate in your own expression of "Like you, know you, trust you, buy from you," the stronger your energetic strength is. It can be used as another mirror of your biz and of you Inner Game.

I just got back from a morning with Alexandra Brown, the E-Zine Queen of the early 2000s. I had heard many good things about her but not paid any attention. People love her and she demonstrated how she arranges that. I am learned from her.

Alexandra is a master of arranging things so people engage in liking her, knowing her, trusting her and then buying from her. I realize Oprah did a very similar thing. Both women tell compelling personal stories and strive to be self-revealing about their personal lives. In her ezines Alexandra always shares something about her personal life and often a photo. She has shared about her cats with cat photos. This has netted her surprising sales. There is much more to the cat story and its uses I have notes on.

Loving people by itself is not enuf to make sales if you believe in relationship selling. You have to also share your inner self. It's not what you know or about your integrity; it's opening up to people so they can "see your guts" and perceive "He/she's like me,"

This signals the inner child of your customers to make an equation, "I'm on of his/her people; he/she's one of my people."

The key to the success of both Alexandra Brown and Oprah, and perhaps other stars you can think of, is

HealingToolbox.org

intimacy. They allow, promote and create a feeling of connection and intimacy with their audiences and do not exploit or manipulate. They ask us for our hearts and they behave as trustworthy keepers of our affection.

Let's detour into intimacy here as it's a crucial aspect of how you win at the Inner Game of Success.

Intimacy as "into-me-see"

Intimacy is the thing we crave most as human beings. And yet a tremendous paradox exists in that intimacy is a commodity virtually no one gets as much of as they wish to; and, virtually no one has any great abundance of--in their own estimation.

Complicating matters we all fantasize a lot about how much intimacy other people have. We often label marriage and raising children as successful "intimate relationships." However we know from the rate of divorce—the participants would often disagree with our assessment.

We are very prone to project our fantasy of intimacy fulfilled onto couples and parents with children because we have little or no information about how much intimacy actually occurs and what each party thinks and feels about the quality of their intimacy. Eric Berne, the founder of Transactional Analysis, estimated in one of his books, around 1965, that the average normal person has no more than five minutes of truly loving intimacy with another human being in their entire lifetime.

So the paradox continues. At the same time intimacy is the thing we most want--it is also the thing we fear most--because the other person "holds up a mirror" in which we see ourselves--and--we may not like our own reflection.

Intimacy can be scary because someone else will also be more able to see into us. Having someone see deeply into me, all of me, behind the facade I hold up to the world--can really rock your boat if your habit has been avoiding your own sub- and unconscious feelings, thoughts and memories.

What Alexandra Brown and Oprah demonstrate is capacity for allowing other people in, allowing other people into their lives; and then, inviting them to participate in the products and services they offer.

This sums up the entire topic of "Relationship Selling" pretty succinctly. Readers will also notice how far this idea of selling is inside the traditional feminine camp of values and activity, how far away it is outside the traditional masculine camp of values and activities To use terms from The NEW Energy Anatomy, it is left-sided, into-me-see, relationship selling, transparency about who you are, is primarily a left-sided activity

Find a full discussion of our right and left sides as two sides of seeing, as two sides of abundance, as two sides of receptivity in the Energy Anatomy book also.

HealingToolbox.org

Back to Alexandra Brown. In her ezines she always shares something about her personal life and often a very recent photo or two or three. She shares photos of her cat, of her cat with a tiny birthday hat on not looking too happy. This picture, she says, netted her over one hundreds buys of a high ticket item; presumably, from pet lovers—who also love Alexandra.

Want a more dramatic example of opening up to into-me-see that had the side-effect of increasing buys by customers?

In the mid-1980s I attended a Conference of 1000 people hosted by John-Roger and his org. In his concluding talk of the Conference, he told the personal story of the passing of his father from colon cancer. His father wanted to die at home and had an open cancer wound eating him out from the inside, requiring home nursing care. John-Roger told about Phil Anthony, one of his staff, who was visiting John-Roger and the dying father. Apparently the nurse was not on duty and the father was uncomfortable. Phil patiently and willingly cleaned out his father's cancer wound. J-R was very moved by Phil's service to his father and in retelling it, cried about it openly. This story, this very emotional scene, went on for about 20 minutes in the Conference talk, in public, before a crowd of about 1000. It was received as an unrehearsed, truly personal sharing. Many of us felt closer to John-Roger after this sharing than we had before. I don't think a recording was ever publicly released. It was pretty raw.

HealingToolbox.org

At the end of the seminar I compared notes with a friend. I told him, "This means personal-spiritual growing is all about becoming completely human." My friend agreed.

In other words, a very valuable approach to marketing any holistic health services is opening up to people so they can see what you are like on the inside and perceive "he's like me," or, "she's like me." If they like what they see, then they conclude, "I'm one of his people; he's one of my people." John-Roger has done this magnificently, in my opinion, for the people he wishes to reach.

If we now go back to simplified one-dimensional marketing terms; we have, like-ability. Practice being likable.

Greater success always feels surreal at first

If my current success is 3/10; which is normal and average here on Earth, your current manifestation of your success is 30% of what it could be, against a hypothetical optimum.

Consider this fantasy. If tomorrow you moved up to success at 8/10, that would more than double your present success. How would that feel? "Surreal" is how this would feel. Imagine how 8/10 would feel very different from 4/10.

NLP trainers like Tony Robbins keep encouraging us to increase our exploration of our sensory channels and arrange things so enthusiasm flows into and thru our sensory images of success. This necessary shift is required to move forward rapidly in your success expression. Greater success has to, must, feel different than the success you have today. Our collection of habits and memories on all levels, physical, imaginal, emotional, mental and mythological—our habit body, is used to success at 3/10. If it moves up to 8/10, many of your comfort zones will be impacted. Greater success is always going to feel different, unfamiliar, a bit strange. You can GET USED TO THIS.

Experiments to verify neck-up and neck-down are different for you

Pick something you like: food, movie, book, music. This is your "target."

Measure how much you like your target first from the neck up.

Then measure how much you like it again, from the neck down.

Are the two numbers the same or different?

Example of mine ~ Watch Dark Souls 2 video game walkthroughs on YouTube:

Neck-up = 8/10.

Neck-down = 1/10.

This is why I don't have a video game console to play these; on the other hand, I do occasionally watch walkthroughs online to wind down before bed.

The response from the neck up tells your rational mind's point of view towards your target.

The response from the neck down expresses your inner child's point of view towards that same target.

A typical difference is quite large. I'm going to bet you your two numbers are different; often, way different.

Q: WHY are my two numbers so way different?

A: Because you have TWO perspectives, not just one. This is natural. Your two perspectives can be different, seeing life from two dissimilar angles; more technically, from two different frequency levels.

Measuring anything from both the neck up and the neck down, is often educational. It can correct many inaccurate, mostly partial-incomplete inner pictures of what's going on inside our own psyche.

Making two measures, above and below the neck, gives a more accurate picture of how we do the things we do and how we like the things we like.

Experiment 2 ~

How good am I at adding, subtracting, multiplying and dividing numbers neck-up~neck-down?

Neck-up = ___/10.

Neck-down = ____/10.

Experiment 3 ~

How good am I at riding a bicycle neck-up~neck-down?

Neck-up = ____/10.

Neck-down = ____/10.

The above experiments suggest how different activities rate differently neck-up and neck-down— and this is so. Different parts of you are talented at different tasks.

Neck-up~neck-down do not both have to be good at all the same things. They are a TEAM, each with unique strengths.

Head to foot, you have a team of FOUR frequencies.

In the Inner Family, Inner Court and heart muscle we will see other teams of four worth stabilizing, balancing and harmonizing so they can work as more effective teams.

The Angelic Plan is for all teams of four to work together. You might recall something about the four Archangels. Same things I think.

Conclusion

Can you see how the above material can be used as tools to build rapport with the inner child? I sure hope so.

Can you see how the above material can be used as tools to work with clients on their goals? I hope so.

Can you see how the above material can be used to facilitate "Coaching as a Conversation for greater inner and outer Mobility"? That's Timothy Gallwey's phrase from *The Inner Game of Work* (Random House, 2001). You can see part of his chapter on this at Google Books. Adding dowsing or testing to the subject expands any "conversation for mobility" way beyond what talk alone can do.

Can you see how the above material can be used to explore the question: How, in what way, can Spirit flow thru me more fully now?

   Exercises are included here for you to do. I hope you will do them. I invite you to contact me with your results and learnings so we can make the next edition of this book better. Exercises here increase in complexity as you read thru this "manual" so be sure to do the early ones.
This is a walk and a swim in the shallow end of the swimming pool. You can into deeper waters at your own discretion. Let's wade into the shallow end.

Your body is the bridge between you and Spirit

Your Body Is the Bridge between the "little you" and "bigger you."
Sooner or later--you will find a version of self-muscle-testing, appealing to you. This will be you, setting your foot, on a path of self-mastery, a path you choose.

>Final words: "Always Use Love All Ways"

>Walk no path

>that does not have loving on it

>at the beginning,

>on the way and at the end.

>\v\V/v/

APPENDICES

Only way to change something in a mirror--is to change yourself

A crucial topic for all holistic practitioners is playing the Inner Game of Success. Profitability here is usually the difference between sustainable, profitable holistic enterprise and a hobby.

How do you play? You accept the possibility your biz is a mirror of your life, a mirror of your personal strengths and weaknesses. The more closely you identify with your biz, the more strongly your biz will reflect your life; therefore, the inner game of business is especially pointed for persons striving to live a holistic lifestyle of any kind.

This is why so many successful entrepreneurs walk a path of personal and/or spiritual growth.

The holistic-green-spiritual the entrepreneur's product-services are, the more often you will see them devoting time and attention to their own growing.

I knew this when I first went full time as a Health Intuitive in private practice. One of the very first things I did was hire a coach in Medical Intuition, Mimi Castellanos (HealthyEnergetics.net).

I picked her following the advice to get someone at the next stage more successful than I in my same field.

Our twice-monthly sessions together opened my eyes further how my biz mirrored my life. As we cleared up negativity in my sub- and unconscious, my relations with self, other people, the world and how I connected with my own Divinity--all expanded and improved. My session work with clients improved directly in proportion to clearing of personal negativity in my sub- and unconscious. I gained ability to hear the inner rhythms of clients and was able to apply to session work, the keys I had gained in my own self-healing.

So I was lucky. I had very low resistance to engaging in the Inner Game of Success.

So the paradox continues. At the same time "intimacy" is the thing we most want--it is also the thing we fear most.

Why? Because another person "holds up a mirror" in which we see ourselves--and--we may not like our own reflection.

Intimacy can be scary because someone else will also be more able to see into us. Having someone see deeply into me, all of me, behind the facade I hold up to the world--can really rock your boat if your habit is avoiding your own child within.

Mirror Game fairy tale

I accept the possibility my biz is a mirror of my life, a mirror of my personal strengths and weaknesses.

The more strongly your self-esteem and self-concept are identified with your biz, the more strongly your biz reflects your life.

If your biz is a mirror and you don't like the reflection, how do you fix a problem in the mirror? You have to change yourself before the mirror can change.

How do you change your reflection in a mirror?
Fairy Tale

HealingToolbox.org

This reminds me of a fairy tale, the fairy tale of the mirror.

Once upon a time there was a princess, in a big castle, locked up in the attic, at the top of a tall tower. She longed to get out and move freely about again--but she could not. When she was younger, the princess had displeased a witch.

The witch pointed to the Princesses' arrogance, impatience and intolerance. The witch put her under a spell. The curse was she had to find a way to change the image in a magic mirror placed in the attic room. The Princess could not understand what to do! Every time she looked into the mirror, all she was her regular self, nothing different. How could she change what the mirror reflected?

Until she could change the image in her mirror, she was locked inside the room, imprisoned and immobilized.

The Princess looked in the mirror every day. Over time, she grew not to like what she saw; she no longer enjoyed her own reflection. She did not like what she looked like to the outer world. Still, she had no idea how to change how she looked inside the mirror.

Over time she felt imprisoned both by the castle tower and by her own reflection in the mirror, an image that would not change and which she could not escape.

Ah! If only you could have been there, Dear Reader, to give her hope and tell her she was imprisoned by her own arrogance, impatience and intolerance. Alas you were not. The Princess had to discover this for herself. Here's how she did it.

One day, the mirror, which had been silent so far, began talking back to her. "I don't like you. You don't treat me very well."

Huh? Who was this talking? It looked like her own self but it said things she had never heard before. "I don't know what you are talking about? What do you mean?"

"Every time you look at me, you criticize what I look like. You tell me all the things I am doing wrong. You never complement me on what I do right. You never celebrate my successes. You are impatient when I can't do what you want me to do. You want everything right away. You only want what you want, when you want it. You don't care about me."

The mirror spoke this way to the Princess; every day, for a long time. Since she had no choice and no one else to talk with, gradually the Princess learned to listen to her Mirror.

She began to hear her own voice talking to her, a voice from deeper inside than her familiar rational mind. She accepted she was hearing, for the first time, from her silent partner, a voice that had been silent up to now. The mirror told her what her feeling mind was feeling. Trapped as she was, she had no choice but to listen.

Finally the Princess asked her mirror a better question. "Mirror, can you help me break the curse so I can get out of this trap? How do I break the curse?"

The mirror spoke, "Easy. But you'll never do it."

"No! Please tell me, I'll listen!"

"Do you really want to hear how to break the curse?"

"Yes, yes, truly, with all my heart!" The Princess in the mirror unfolded her crossed arms and tried to make herself look more open-minded and agreeable.

"Well if you really want to know how to break the spell, all you have to do is work with me so that you and I are partners and do things together."

The Princess gulped, "How do I do that?"

"Consult with me for a second opinion on choices and decisions especially those that pertain to food-diet-nutrition, sleep, exercise, and emotions."

"I can do that."

"It also means not assuming I understand what you mean when you have an idea. You have to ASK me.

You can't assume I'm in agreement with you; YOU HAVE TO ASK.

It means we work together, as partners, choosing many more of our little steps forward in life. "

HealingToolbox.org

"I can do that; oh, I promise, I PROMISE!"

The princess in the mirror folded her arms again. "Not good enuf. I don't trust you. We need something, a little ritual, to help you keep our agreement uppermost in your mind. To demonstrate your willingness to partner with me, when you get out of this castle attic, whenever you look into any mirror of any kind, you will see me. I'll be looking at you. If I'm smiling, you will know you have my trust and cooperation and that we are working together as a team."

"How will this be different from how I have always looked into mirrors?"

The princess in the mirror wagged her finger. "No, checking your hair, teeth and clothes in a mirror is not partnering with me. From now on you will NOT look into a mirror to check how your body looks to other people. From now on when you look into a mirror, you will look for me, your silent partner, and you will check how we are doing as a team.

"If you see happiness, we are together. If you see anything else, our relationship needs your attention ASAP!"

"You want connection with me, mutual respect and appreciation—not simply me looking good to others. Okay, I can do that."

"If you start partnering with me and remain cooperative with me, the tower door will fling open and you will no longer feel imprisoned by what you see in any mirror."

HealingToolbox.org

So the real Princess promised to partner with her silent partner in the mirror and ask her for her opinion frequently.

The lock on the tower door just fell off. The Princess was free to leave the attic and rejoin other people!

At first it was new for the Princess to remember to ask her silent partner for a second opinion. Her technique for communicating with her silent partner improved as she practiced. From that time on, every time she looked into a mirror, she saw a warm, open smiling face, a very attractive and interesting face. No one could have taught the Princess this. She had to learn it her self.

She noticed had to practice or the connection tended to fade. It was "use it or lose it" situation.

No part of staying in touch with her self was too difficult. It was more like a healthy self-discipline. She only had to remember to ask her silent partner for its opinion one more time than she forgot. This process helped her to slow down and take time for her feeling mind.

It didn't matter exactly HOW she communed with her image in the mirror. This changed from day to day and was flexible. The only wrong way to do it seemed to be not to try at all.

As she and her mirror image became more and more harmonious, the Princess began receiving compliments from both friends and strangers about how good she looked; she liked that.

HealingToolbox.org

She also noticed how few other people around her smiled. She wondered if they had partnerships with their own reflections. Other people looked into mirrors but only seemed to check their hair, their makeup, how they looked to others--not to them self.

Over time, the Princess learned to slow down any time she felt she was of two minds. She would find a convenient mirror and have a talk with her feeling mind self. Together they worked out a course of action agreeable to both of them not just to one or the other.

So the TWO of them lived happily ever after; and, if things haven't changed, they're still the same today.

~ THE END ~

Moral: How do you change your reflection in a mirror? You have to change yourself before mirrors reflecting you can change.

Playing the Inner game, seeing your biz clearly, means seeing your SELF clearly. It pays off for me to accept my biz mirrors my life, mirroring my personal strengths and weaknesses. "Failure is only feedback" as John Maguire says. When I feel blocked in achieving my goals, I take a breath * sigh * and realize, yes, I must be OUT of congruence with myself. Then I can learn which game, Inner or Outer, needs my attention now.

HealingToolbox.org

The Outer Game of Manifestation is always reflecting our Inner Game of Light. It can't be any other way!

The more closely you identify with your biz--the more strongly your biz will reflect your life. This may be the best argument of all for maintaining a healthy firewall between your business and your personal life!

Inner Game Exercise:

Likability self-test

There is no way to prosperity; prosperity is the way ~ Wayne Dyer (found in Debbie Bermont's Outrageous Business Growth book)

Many readers will know the sales formula: first the customer learns to like you; then they learn to know you better; then they learn to trust you; when they do and they are ready to buy, they buy from you.

Did you know you can test and measure these?

If you wish, have a partner do arm-pull-down on you where you--and only you--determine the meaning of the following.

Use a scale of 1-10 for all of these, 1 = hardly at all, 10 = optimal for me today.

HealingToolbox.org

I like myself the way I am. _____/10

I know myself well. _____/10

I trust myself now. _____/10

I would buy from me now. _____/10

Find some high numbers? Please celebrate!

Find some low numbers? This is where improvement is possible, blocks and obstacles possible to address. I wonder what you will set in motion to address these...

Q: Help! I found several low numbers! What do I do!

A: See "What to do if you find a low number" below.

Faulty beliefs to self-assess

If you don't stand for something, you will fall for anything ~ Malcom X (found in Debbie Bermont's *Outrageous Business Growth* book)

More complete discussion of using scales. Measuring and algebra in self-testing appears in the forthcoming, *Math, Scales, Geometry, Pre-algebra in Energy Medicine Clearing*

Extra blank space appears below each one so you can revise it to what is true for you now.

It's okay to be successful, just not TOO successful

It's okay to be successful, just not more successful than my parents... than other family members... than someone else I know.

People don't applaud my success; they scheme for my demise.

Don't get too big for your britches.

Life is a struggle.

Life is supposed to be hard, you suffer, then you die. That's it.

If I don't have problems, I don't feel alive.

If things go well, watch out, something bad is coming around the corner.

There is not enough, not enuf for everyone.

I don't deserve to get my share.

If I don't do it perfectly, I will fail.

I'm not ready yet.

I need to study and learn more first.

I have to know ahead of time if this will work.

HealingToolbox.org

Above beliefs slightly adapted from the *Power of YOU* by Scott Martineau, a wonderful tennis coach in Rancho Palos Verdes, CA.

"My body tightens up…" experiment

When I imagine being more successful, where I tighten up in my body is _____.

"It's easy for me" self-assessments

It's easy for me to share the value of my products-service.

It's easy for me to be the kind of person people want to buy from.

It's easy for me to be the kind of person people want to buy my product-service from.

It's easy for me to attract and keep new high-value, long-term clients.

It's easy for me to attract, keep and pay assistants who like to do the tasks I am not good at.

It's easy for me to identify, learn from and become like healthy role models of people successful in my exact field-speciality.

I'm naturally lucky. It's easy for me to ask for the right thing, at the right time, within my highest good, which is possible, permitted and clear for me now.

Prosperity beliefs for self- assessing

A scale of 1-10, ten being optimal for you today, is recommended.

Each of these can be measured on a scale of ten-out-of-ten as optimal for you today.

* I trust myself to manage money honestly and sensibly.

* It is okay for me to make mistakes with money.

* Money is one expression of my spirituality, my love for God, myself and others.

* I am calm and confident when I have money.

* I am calm and confident when I do not have money.

* I deserve to have all the money I need.

Personal Power beliefs to self-assess

* I trust the decisions I make.

* I trust Divine guidance I am receiving.

* I acknowledge my ability and responsibility to make a positive difference in the world.

* I actively embrace the opportunities that come with change.

* I take initiative to create my life the way I want it.

* I am true to my personal vision.

Self-Esteem beliefs you can self-test

* I deeply appreciate and accept myself.

* I forgive myself and all imperfect acts and thoughts, past, present and future.

* I love myself unconditionally.

* I love all aspects of my mind.

* I love all parts of my body.

* I accept my imperfections as opportunities to learn valuable lessons in my life.

* I do my best and my best is good enough.

Spirituality beliefs to self-assess

* It's easy for me to connect with my own Divinity.

* I am a necessary part of the Divine plan.

* My body is a temple of God.

* My Higher Self loves me.

* Every one of my experiences brings me closer to God.

* My life is a perfect demonstration of the principle of Divine Love.

Grief/Loss beliefs you can self-test

* I release the painful past and I eagerly look forward to the good that awaits me now.

HealingToolbox.org

* I release my previous expectations and allow a benevolent universe to support me.

* I have faith that I am being guided to my next step.

* Although I grieve for what I lost, I know that a greater good will follow.

* A new door in my life stands open before me.

When one door closes, another door opens.

Above is excerpted and slightly modified from: http://www.yoursubconsciousbeliefs.com/beliefs.html#dough

Trigger beliefs to self-test

Testing this category of statement challenges us to get more precise and rigorous about our own self-testing. Try setting your intention to test strong if you believe—on any level—the statement at hand:

You have to watch every dime.

I don't want to be like the rich people.

The world is getting worse and worse every day (awfulizing)

You know, it's not safe to let you kids out in the world today.

The love of money is the root of all evil.

Some of us weren't born with talent.

I guess I just wasn't meant for success.

I'm always underpaid.

The government will take it from me.

Lying about money is the only way to keep it.

Negative messages you may have overheard in the womb

- Now we have another mouth to feed; we really have to sacrifice now.

- Oh no, I wasn't planning on this, how will I survive?

- I'm so happy I'm pregnant! I'm going to work hard to make sure the baby has everything they need. (the baby—you--equals "hard work" and "work hard" to earn their right to be here. Can lead to a "Pleaser" personality trying to prove they are "not too much trouble")

- I hope it's a boy/girl I would be really disappointed if it is a boy/girl. (something is wrong with me if I am a boy or a girl.)

The above is adapted and revised from a now-unknown online sales copy.

7 Success beliefs to self-assess

More positive success beliefs you can self-test on. I encourage you to get curious, have courage, and TEST to see if you are strong on each of these. If you test weak on any of these—perhaps a block or obstacle is revealed.

Belief #1: A positive purpose exists behind every event and situation, even if I cannot see it yet

Belief #2: There are only learning experiences, failure is only feedback. If I learned something, I was successful.

Belief #3: Taking personal responsibility is the fastest way to change something you don't like.

Belief #4: I don't need to understand everything perfectly

Belief #5: My biggest resource is my network of relationships and my support people

Belief #6: Work can be play, I allow, create and promote this!

Belief #7: Outer success measures my internal Coherence, Integration and Alignment (CIA).

Excerpted and adapted from Frederic Premji under Success at this site:

http://www.ineedmotivation.com/blog/2008/10/the-seven-beliefs-of-success/

Five Personal Needs to self-assess from Wm. Glasser

I met Dr. William Glasser (http://wglasser.com/) once or twice in person at college, CSUDH, 1991-1993. He was the first person to get me thinking systematically about needs.

Glasser authored the earlier *Reality Therapy* (1969). *Choice Theory* (1998) updates his ideas and culminates his 50 year exploration of the psyche and counseling for the purposes of mental-emotional sanity. Many of his insights were based on hands-on work with troubled and incarcerated teenagers. *Choice Theory* remains one of few 20th century psych books that has not dated much. It still has much to contribute to NVC and to Energy Medicine.

Choice Theory posits basic inborn preferences, based on needs, motivate our behavior.

Here's Glasser's original formulation of five universal needs:

- Survival ~ Breathing, water, food, clothing, shelter, personal safety.
- Love and belonging ~ Intimacy, connection, affection, touching
- Power ~ Influence with & over your peers
- Freedom ~ Set your own goals, control your own time
- Fun ~ Novelty, laughter and celebrations.

Glasser's five inborn needs build on Maslow's earlier hierarchy of needs, also in need of some updating.

Choice Theory says any choices represent a person's best attempt to satisfy one or more of their five basic inborn needs.

Q: Can all needs be reduced to just five?

A: Hold that question; it's a good one.

The Choice Theory model challenges earlier stimulus-response (Behaviorism) models of the 1930s-1960s by positing no choice, no decision, is caused by external situations or persons. Find full discussion in *Choice Theory* for those interested.

HealingToolbox.org

Relationships as the source of unhappiness

Choice Theory further posits the source of much unhappiness is failing or failed relationships, with meaningful others: spouses, parents, children, friends & colleagues.

Choice Theory believes much mental illness tracks back to unhappiness from relationships that don't meet our five authentic basic needs.

Glasser was the first I know of to think both holistically and strategically about needs in our sub- and unconscious.

We each satisfy our basic needs by making choices. Glasser says these five need and their relative proportion in individuals, motivate us towards one choice over another.

Glasser's theory explains why two people, in the same situation, make different choices when all other external factors are the same.

Create your own Needs Preference Profile

Choice Theory invites you to guesstimate your own Personal Needs Profile.

Go ahead, rate yourself on each need, five being highest for you. Different needs, different numbers, go for it:

Survival ____/5

Love, intimacy-belonging ___/5

Power-influence with & over peers ___/5

Freedom as set your own goals, control your own time ___/5

Fun/novelty/laughter ___/5

Now get your spouse or significant other to do their own Needs Preference Profile. DON'T show them your Needs Profile until they complete theirs.
Once you have both Profiles, compare them. Glasser and his wife share many patterns. Read their short book to learn:
- The meaning for couples of similar and contrasting sets of numbers,
- How different two profiles have to be before two people are not compatible,
- Which variations between spouses are easier to tolerate than others.
Glasser's book on this is *Getting Together and Staying Together; Solving the Mystery of Marriage* (2000). Available for one-cent here:
http://www.amazon.com/Getting-Together-Staying-Solving-Marriage/dp/006095633X/ref=sr_1_1?ie=UTF8&qid=1363666909&sr=8-1&keywords=Getting+Together+and+Staying+Together%3B+Solving+the+Mystery+of+Marriage

Final words: "Always Use Love All Ways"

Walk no path that does not have loving on it at the beginning, on the way and at the end.

About the Author

Bruce has a series of 16 books, 20 videos and 200 articles on Best Practices in Energy Medicine. Find him at HealingToolbox.org

Bruce co-founded the Holistic Chamber of Commerce in Los Angeles.

Health Intuitive Bruce Dickson shows people how to use their own Inner Dashboard so they can increase their own Inner Sunshine. How? By identifying and removing blocks and obstacles to health and success.

Many ways to connect with your own Guidance exist thru the Skill Ladder of Holistic Self-healing Techniques-Methods-Arts. Everyone who wants to can use Tools That Heal and apply Best Practices in Holistic Self-Healing.

HealingToolbox.org

Tools That Heal Press Booklist

Best Practices in Holistic Self-Healing Series

Resources written by and for self-testers

In all modalities

Tools That Heal composed by and for self-healers and self-muscle-testers in all therapeutic modalities.

HealingToolbox.org ~ 310-280-1176 ~ Gift sessions by phone to find and repair the weak link in your Ring of Success. Practitioners, healers and coaches especially invited to call.

All books written in an interactive, FUN style by a practicing Health Intuitive with training from MSIA, USM, NVC and Waldorf teacher training from Rudolf Steiner College.

All books available in PAPER and EBOOK.

Best Practices in Energy Medicine Series

The two best sellers:

3) *Meridian Metaphors,* Psychology of the Meridians and Major Organs

HealingToolbox.org

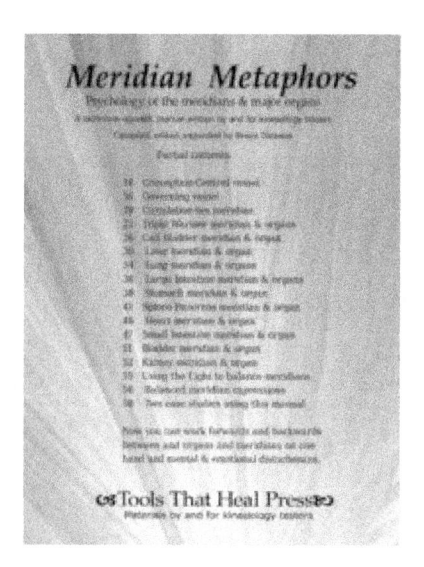

Ever wonder what the connection between meridians, organs and emotions is? Ever think TCM had a start on good ideas but much was missing? Now anyone can work either forwards or backwards, between disturbed organs and meridians on one hand; and, disturbed mental-emotional states on the other hand. All descriptions begin with healthy function. Disturbances are further categorized by under- and overcharge conditions. Includes the myths and metaphors of under- overcharged organs-meridians condensed from Psychological Kinesiology plus much new material from other clinical practitioners. 22,000 words 100 page manual, 8 x10"

11) *The NEW Energy Anatomy:*

Nine new views of human energy that don't require clairvoyance

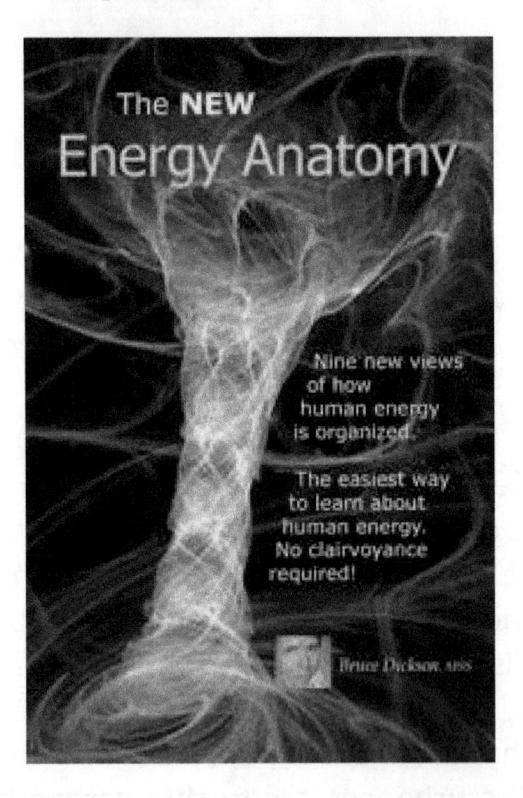

The Three Selves is simply the clearest, easiest map-model for the whole person. Here's the greater detail you would expect in an anatomy that goes with the 3S.

An easier, simpler, faster way to learn about human energy system compared to the chakra system. The NEW Energy Anatomy is a better entry point for students to developing sensitivity. Each view is testable with kinesiology of any and all kinds. You be the judge!

HealingToolbox.org

Physical anatomy is used by every effective energetic practitioner and self-healer. When your target is invisible, as often true--the best map is invaluable!

Maps of chakras, auras, acupuncture points, and reflex points are common—and commonly confusing to students because they cannot be perceived directly without clairvoyance. If you ARE clairvoyant, these aspects are easier to perceive and lead into the even deeper symbology of the chakra system.

These nine simpler views replace the chakra system as a starting place for most students of human energy. Each one is testable with kinesiology of any method. See for yourself!

NEW Energy Anatomy replaces some of the older views of human energy with views much simpler to visualize

Particularly useful for energy school students and sensitive persons using testing to sort out their abundant perceptions. More generally useful for efforts to become more Coherent, Integrated and Aligned (the new CIA). Coupled with Touch for Health, EFT, Energy Medicine or PTS Masters and Doctorate programs, these views facilitate making your aura brighter.

Human energy is organized:

1) Right and left in the body, yin & yang in the body.

2) Top and bottom, enteric and cerebral nervous systems.

3) Front and back, CV-GV, Clark Kent and Superman.

4) As frequency, best viewed as four kinds of laughter!

5) Our gut brain has two frequencies, divided top and bottom, feeling above (hey, hey hey!) and willingness below (ho, ho, ho!).

6) Our inner child has four distinct quadrants, an Inner Court.

7) We have a second Inner Court in our head.

8) The back of our head is willingness to heal our past.

9) Hip stability is a Ring of Loving you can strengthen.

Other material includes the Law of Gentleness for healers, coaches & counselors. 25,000 words 145 p. in 6x9 format.

1) **You have FIVE bodies, PACME, Spiritual Geography 101** (99 cent eBook)

You have FIVE bodies PACME
Spiritual Geography 101

Bruce Dickson, MSS, MA

Tools That Heal Press
Best Practices in Self-Healing System Series
HealingToolbox.org

A fundamental distinction John-Roger and others make early and often is the useful tool of Spiritual Geography, discerning we have not one body here on Earth, but FIVE. Take away or compromise with any one of these bodies and we become less than fully human, less than fully capable of giving and receiving love. Topics include:

What makes us human is primarily invisible

Experience your five bodies RIGHT NOW

Two simple spiritual geographies

The map of Creation in your own hand

HealingToolbox.org

PACME ~ CIEMU: low frequency to high frequency

Tiger's Fang & When Are You Coming Home?

CIEMU can also be concentric circles

We have habits and comfort zones on each level CIEMU

Can I measure the soul here in 3D?

Can I see the soul here in the 3D world?

How does Spirit view my illness?

Where does physical disease come from?

Where are the primary causative factors of illness?

Only two kinds of problems

Why is the outer world more compelling than the inner?

Redeeming the imagination

2) The Meaning of Illness is Now an Open Book;

Cross-referencing Illness and Issues

Virtually unknown to the public, EIGHT excellent, peer-reviewed books exist correlating illnesses and mental-emotional issues as of 2013.

It's now possible to simply look up the meaning of physical illnesses, the causative issues behind health concerns. Some combination of these mental-emotional issues is what oppresses your organs, tissues and cells.

For persons with their own Healing Toolbox, they can simply get busy doing what you can to locate, address and resolve these issues. Muscle testing, kinesiology testing of any kind is the most convenient way to navigate to which issue is "live" in you.

If you don't know where your Healing Toolbox is or what's in it, you can always find a Self-Healing

HealingToolbox.org

Coach, Health Intuitive or Medical Intuitive. Find someone who works with loving.

Those interested in the mental-emotional meaning of illnesses tend to be, self-healers, self-muscle-testers, holistic practitioners, kinesiology practitioners, Medical and Health Intuitives, energy detectives of all kinds and anyone interested in what used to be called "psychosomatic medicine."

Ill-informed, useless and eccentric literature in this field does exist. These are the books I recommend.

Additional material concerns how one Medical Intuitive views his field and his practice:

- Illness as a healing metaphor.

- Willingness to heal is the pre-requisite to heal

- Summary of some very recent protocols and methods for connecting the dots between illnesses and issues.

Chapter Four has some original research on therapeutic metaphors for illness: Cancer and tumors in general, Stroke, SIDS, Autism, Alzheimer's, ADHD, Attention deficit, Hyperactive disorder.

A Proposed Wikipedia page upgrade on "Medical Intuitive"

4) *Your Habit Body,* An Owner's Manual

Our Habit Body is our best and closest friend. It remembers every routine thing we do daily--so we don't have to relearn all our habits all over again each day. Habits are reactivity set on automatic, behavior conditioned to repeat.

If this is so, how come the one thing human beings do better than anything else is to make the same mistake over and over and over again?

Based on results, we don't know as much about our habit body as people think. We need new Tools That Heal to get at the 90% of our habit body that is sub- and unconscious.

We have habits on five personality levels: physical, imaginal, emotional, mental and unconscious. How are they organized? How do we keep all our habits organized so when we wake up in the morning, we don't have to relearn everything? Personal-spiritual growth is upgrading our habits on any of these levels. Sound like a lot to manage? This makes your job easier, the missing manual for anyone who owns a Habit Body.

We used to say, "He who doesn't know his history is doomed to repeat it." We can say more precisely, "Whoever neglects their habit body will have the same behaviors and results tomorrow, as they did yesterday." Find answers here:

- Why we were more lovable when we were young

- Every day we are "training a new puppy"

- Why 90% of habits are invisible in 3D

- A dozen common terms for the "habit body."

Garrison Keillor says, "Culture is what you know is so by age 12." ALL culture can be seen as just a bunch of habits, including your own. Once you can see it, you can redirect it. 78 pages.

5) You are a Hologram Becoming Visible to Your Self

You are a Hologram
Becoming visible to your self

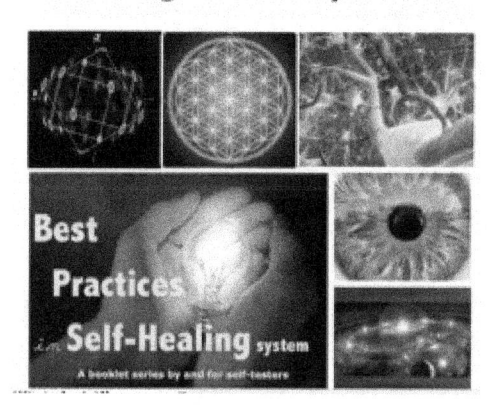

The bigger part of us, our inner child, immune system, high self, "true self," "divine connection"--however you term it, is invisible to us for several reasons--but you can change this and get to know the "bigger you."

The metaphor of a hologram is a good way to see the "bigger you" behind all the familiar smokescreens.

A hologram metaphor assists us to reframe the "bigger you" with new eyes. As modern people, we understand a hologram has both three dimensions and internal structure. These are useful metaphors for our inner dimensions and the structures in our sub- and unconscious. Our psyche is a hologram of physical, imaginal, emotional, mental and mythological potentials. Some are fully activated, many are not. Some are stuck and dysfunctional.

HealingToolbox.org

What we have inside us can be understood in terms of a 3D framework and a hologram is the way to "see" this, the structure of the "bigger you."

A full discussion of how the "bigger you" is structured and organized as a hologram, and the history of this idea, in included in this work.

6) 2nd edition coming 2014 **Self-Healing 101; Seven Experiments in Self-healing You Can Do at Home to Awaken the Inner Healer**

HealingToolbox.org

Self-Healing 101

9 Experiments in self-healing you *can* do at home to Awaken the Inner Healer

Anyone CAN begin to self-heal doing Goethean Holistic experiments on the Skill Ladder of Holistic Self-healing Techniques. Wherever you are is a good place to start. You can start NOW.

Bruce Dickson, Health Intuitive
Best Practices in Self-healing Series
Tools That Heal Press ~ HealingToolbox.org

Anyone CAN self-heal. Wherever you are is a good place to start. You can start NOW

For those looking to go deeper into self-healing and/or begin or deepen their practice of self-muscle-testing. Alternatively, for those teaching others how to self-muscle-test.

Self-healing and self-muscle-testing is outside the exhausted residue of Cartesian-Newtonian Science. Self-healing and self-muscle-testing is really part of the more appropriate newer Goethean Holistic Science; that is, all results, all phenomena, are replicable but NOT by all persons, at all places and all times, regardless of intention. Rather results are replicable primarily in the domain of one person.

Q: How do I begin our own journey of self-healing in the domain of one person, myself?

A: We move to a more experiential approach to self-healing beginning with

- Self-acceptance, self-love

- prayers of self-protection

- self-sensitivity

- self-permission to make testing experiments.

In hands-on Goethean Holistic Science experiments, there is no penalty for failure, none at all--as long-- as you learn something from every experiment.

The only wrong way to experiment is not to try at all.

7) "Willingness to heal is the pre-requisite for all healing"

"Willingness to heal is the prerequisite for all healing"

Reactivity

Best Practices in Healing 400 level material

Willingness to Heal

Bruce DiGloss, LPC, LLC

Tools That Heal Press
Best Practices in Healing
Resources by and for kinesiology testers

This quote from Bertrand Babinet begins exploration and expansion of some of Bertrand Babinet's wonderful legacy of theory and method.

If you can do kinesiology testing by any method, you can measure your own willingness to heal. Self-testers can measure their own willingness to heal, in your inner child.

This tells you if your silent partner is ready to heal what you wish to heal. You can use this to explore where you are most ready to grow.

Have clients? The effectiveness of any energetic session can be estimated AHEAD OF TIME, with surprising accuracy--before you begin working!

HealingToolbox.org

Practitioners in any and all modalities, are encouraged measure willingness to heal FIRST!

Save your self from wasting effort when clients are of two minds on their issue and do not know this. The higher the number on a scale of 1-10, the more momentum your client has to heal on that issue.

Willingness to heal is the key to aligning and integrating the three selves. Willingness is where the whole topic of the 3S leads.

NOTE ~ This booklet assumes readers can already either self-test using kinesiology testing—K-testing, dowsing, or some other form; or, can follow instructions to use any partner to do two-person testing, termed Client

Controlled Testing. Problems with your own testing? Don't trust your own results? See the training protocol breakthroughs in Self-Healing 101.

8) *You Have Three Selves;* Simplest, clearest model of the Whole Person, Volume ONE, Orientation

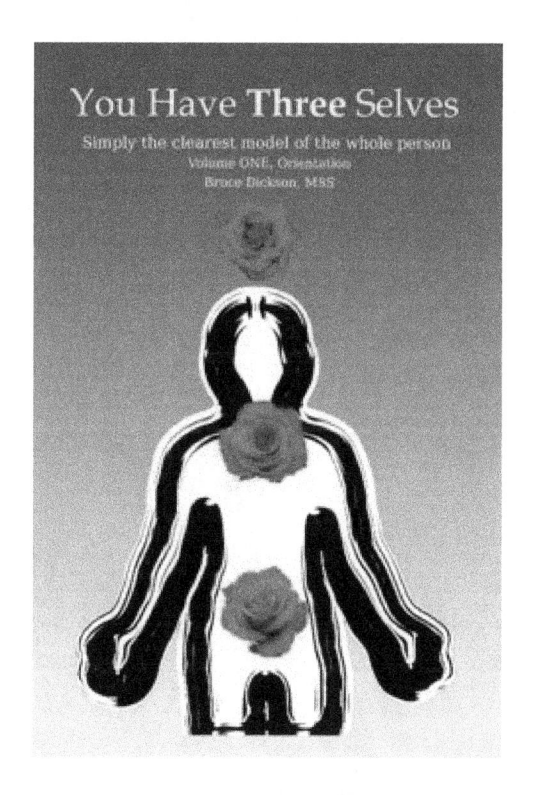

Compose your own vision of self-healing with the first comprehensive general textbook on the Three Selves. The basic self is functionally equal to the inner child, Little Artist, immune system and 12 other 20th century terms. The conscious self is your rational mind, which can be either feeling or thinking! Your high self is your guardian angel, your own higher Guidance. Aligning all three of these on the same goal so they can work as a team, describes much of what we do in 3D embodiment. Written with diagrams and much humor. 223 p. 6x9"

HealingToolbox.org

9) *You Have Three Selves*; Simplest, clearest model of the Whole Person; Volume TWO, Finding the 3S in Your Life

If the Three Selves are universal and pervasive in psychology, they ought to be visible all around us. Yikes, it's true! Find the 3S in your body, in pop culture, in the fun of Transactional Analysis, etc. 93 p. 6x9"

10) COMING 2014: Muscle Testing as a Spiritual Exercise;

HealingToolbox.org

Building a Bridge to Your Body's Wisdom

Muscle Testing as a Spiritual Exercise
Building a Bridge to Your Body's Wisdom

- Muscle-Testing Redesigned for 'God is my Partner'

- How to tune into the "bigger you"

- Making healthier choices is for everyone

Bruce Dickson, MSS, MA
Tools That Heal Press ~ Healing Toolbox.org

- Muscle-Testing Redesigned for 'God is my Partner'

- How to tune into the "bigger you"

- Making healthier choices is for everyone

The Healing Toolbox approach to "how to do muscle testing."

I began writing this book around 2001. Why the long gestation? Almost the whole modern history of muscle testing had to be stood on its head, everything I had learned from dowsing and then Touch for Health. Conventional approach to muscle testing had to be DIS-connected from Cartesian-Newtonian science; then, plugged into Goethean Holistic Science. Consequently, this is NOT your mother's-father's kinesiology manual.

22 videos are also referenced and their topics are expanded on here.

Our small intestine is already muscle testing 24/7. As waking-conscious selves, we can re-arrange our thinking to use this to our advantage. It requires some lively conceptual ju-jitsu. I believe the journey will be both practical and entertaining.

ANY method on the Skill Ladder of Holistic Self-healing Techniques-Methods-Arts is useful on a Heroes Journey of Self-healing. Cessation of inner againstness and releasing of outworn "stories" PACME is always good.

The Skill Ladder is here: "A clear skill ladder exists of holistic self-healing methods-techniques-arts" http://www.healingtoolbox.org/k2-stub/item/333-skill-ladder-of-holistic-healing-methods-techniques-arts

This book address primarily only the technique-method-art of self-muscle-testing.

Arm-length-testing is preferred for beginners over all other methods. Any other method of muscle testing is fine too. Arm-length-testing is here: http://innerwise.com/en/videos/all-videos/113-innerwise-the-arm-lenght-test?category_id=54

12) COMING 2014

Measuring, math and scales--with 'God as my Partner

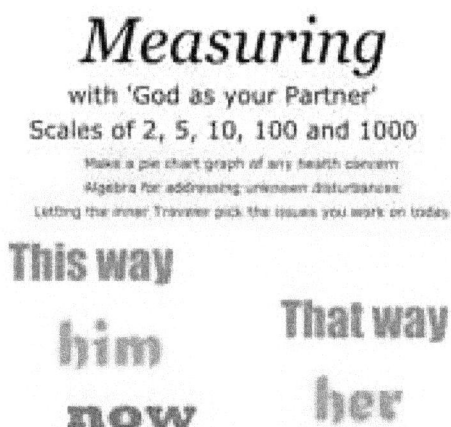

Measuring
with 'God as your Partner'
Scales of 2, 5, 10, 100 and 1000

Make a pie chart graph of any health concern
Algebra for addressing unknown disturbances
Letting the inner Traveler pick the issues you work on today

This way him now X

That way her then Y

Best Practices in Self-Healing System
A booklet series by and for self-testers & Healing Buddies

Many Goethean Science experiments in self-testing to explore, experiment and expand skills in self-healing. Written for dowsers, self-testers, self-healers and those wishing to improve their self-testing.

ALL exercises here REQUIRE familiarity and/or some skill with muscle testing, kinesiology testing, dowsing.

If you like and dislike things, you are already measuring invisible--still real things. Every time you choose one option over another, you are measuring invisibles.

You measure if the weather is too hot or too cold to wear this or that clothing. If you sing, you are constantly measuring to stay on key. If you dance, you are constantly measuring if your are following the rhythm or not. All these things are invisible.

May as well get good at measuring invisibles, we do it every day.

When we add scales and numbers to our unconscious measuring exercises, we include, train and strengthen the conscious-waking self.

With children, after age seven, to support their conscious self, we encourage accurate counting of physical items via math manipulatives.

For adults, counting invisible things precisely is mostly called "muscle testing," sometimes "dowsing." Muscle testing of any kind strengthens the conscious self even more quickly than math manipulatives because we are attending to real things that while unseen, are still countable.

The healthy human being is the primary and sometimes only accurate measuring tool for measuring character, as we do in voting, elections and mate selection. May as well get good at it!

13) *The Inner Court: Close-up of the Habit Body*

The Inner Court
Close-up of the habit body
How Guinevere, Lancelot, Merlin & Arthur influence you every day

Bruce Dickson, MSS

Building on Your Habit Body, An Owner's Manual, our gut brain (inner child) is shown to have four quadrants. This is the next logical level deeper than the inner child, the beginning of the Fractal Personality.

The four archetypal characters of Camelot, Guinevere, Lancelot, Merlin & King Arthur (GLMA) have long-served as lenses for insight into our own subconscious role playing. Add muscle testing, and you can use them to navigate your habit body to what is working and not working in your psyche. It becomes possible to see where our habits,

HealingToolbox.org

behaviors, and comfort zones are running, repeating and where we can make changes.

Functional~dysfunctional expressions of each member of the Inner Court are provided. This erects a body-centric map to locate where everyday disturbances originate and track back to. If you can feel it—and locate it--you can heal it!

All aspects of the Inner Court lends itself highly to muscle testing experiments.

The Inner Court is a "magic mirror," reflecting our preferred memories, habits and behaviors in body image, posture, attire, accessories and so on.

These four are the KEY ACTORS in our habit body, acting out preferences, memories, habits and behaviors. They are the "script writers," script holders, and role-playing actors, "holding court" in our sub- and unconscious. They determine our habitual memories, habits, behaviors, routines and preferences.

Q: What's left for ME to do?

A: YOU remain Director of this UNconscious "writers room" and acting company.

Soul is choice; nothing determines our personality—unless we allow it. However, we rely on the acquired habits of our Inner Court to suggest how to respond to life situations. If we do not change how we respond, we WILL respond in the habitual ways our Inner Court knows to respond.

HealingToolbox.org

Say you are feeling bad. You can ask, Who inside me feels unresolved? Oh, it's Guinevere! She feels rejected. Let's see why she feels that way and what she needs."

The health and strength of each quadrant is easily assessed and measured with kinesiology testing, muscle testing, of any kind.

These insights have been extensively tested by the author in client sessions since 2001. Insights gleaned from the Inner Court easily transfer to working with clients.

Bertrand Babinet's original names for each quadrant was, Mother, Child, Grandparent, Father.

Readers familiar with Virginia Satir's Stress Response Stances will see the connection and one of the likely origins here.

The Inner Court IS the inner child, in a four-fold, close-up view. It's a more exact, body-based, imagining of "inner child, four times more precise. This map of inner child is four times as precise as Bradshaw's unitary concept of the "inner child."

Arthurian legend always had, always was, a map, a guide, to possible behaviors and expressions possible in the human experience, both functional and dysfunctional.

The map does not determine the territory; the Inner Court does not determine personality. Yet, our every possible like & dislike, strength & weakness, are all "programmed" into the firmware of our habit body. The Inner Court is how to view them so you can learn from and initiate change as you see fit. If you can access a dysfunctional habit, there is Grace available to redirect, upgrade, change or release it.

The purpose of the Inner Family in the gut is highly involved with developing healthy self-esteem from conception to age 11. Before puberty, the locus of control in our psyche is our gut brain in theta. After puberty, locus of control shifts from gut to head brain-spine. The relative activity and interaction of self-esteem and self-concept, presages personality.

Further into our Fractal Psyche, we have TWO Inner Courts, one in our gut brain, a second one in the four brain quadrants. Our cerebral cortex, also has four discernible quadrants but in different order and in a plane turned 90 degrees from the gut brain.

The archetypes of Arthurian legend in the head are highly tied with developing self-concept.

The two Courts make the previously mysterious topics of self-esteem and self-concept understandable.

Q: What is the goal of a quadrant?

A: The goal for each is acknowledgement, safety, trust, connection, cooperation, mutual support and teamwork with the other three in its system. The strength and weakness of relationships between any two members is easy to measure. In this, the Inner Court is the beginning of the Inner Dashboard, the safe and appropriate place for us to work to make changes in our own psyche.

In the six possible relationships between the four archetypes, our personal failures, confusions and successes are expressed and can be easily diagrammed towards understanding our behavior.

The Inner Court makes obvious the strengths and weaknesses of many previous mysteries:

- The limitations of "right and left brain" are completed here in a quadrant system,

- Personality typology in general is clarified,

- The connection between neurotransmitter production and the Inner Court becomes clear,

- The classic Supporter, Promoter, Analyzer, Controller typologies,

- MBTI ideas of how personality is formed thru preferences,

- Aristotle's & Rudolf Steiner's four Temperaments,

- The pioneering work of Ned Herrmann & Katherine Benziger is clarified and made more artistic.

The Inner Court model is appropriate to grad students and ANYONE interested in counseling, coaching, training, sales and personal growth. 116 p. 6x9"

14) The Five Puberties, a Three Selves Journal on Children

You Have Five Puberties
A Three Selves journal on Children
The Three Selves in stage-development terms

Bruce Dickson, MSS, MA

Growing new eyes to see children and stage-development afresh is the goal of this booklet. It builds on the foundation of the other volumes—or--can be read alone. Children are viewed thru lenses not often used: body posture, stories the body tells, animals, plants, the succession of puberties--at least four puberties--each of us undergoes on our journey towards independent thinking.

Finally, we glance at what progress has been made towards a functional typology of children's temperaments in Anthroposophy, MBTI and Katherine Benziger, providing some directions for fruitful further study. The perplexing problem of how children's typology differs from adult typology, is brought close to resolution.

HealingToolbox.org

15) Radical Cellular Wellness—Especially for Women

Cell psychology for everyone; a coherent theory of illness and wellness.

Finally a Theory of Illness and a Theory of How We Heal for everyone—especially for women: your cells are born healthy; and left on their own, cells remain healthy and reproduce perfectly. It is only environmental and human pollution that interferes with cell health and reproduction.

HealingToolbox.org

The various forms of internal pollution we allow, promote and create are discussed with an eye to solutions!

Works incidental & complementary to Best Practices Series, above

- Rudolf Steiner's Fifth Gospel in Story Form

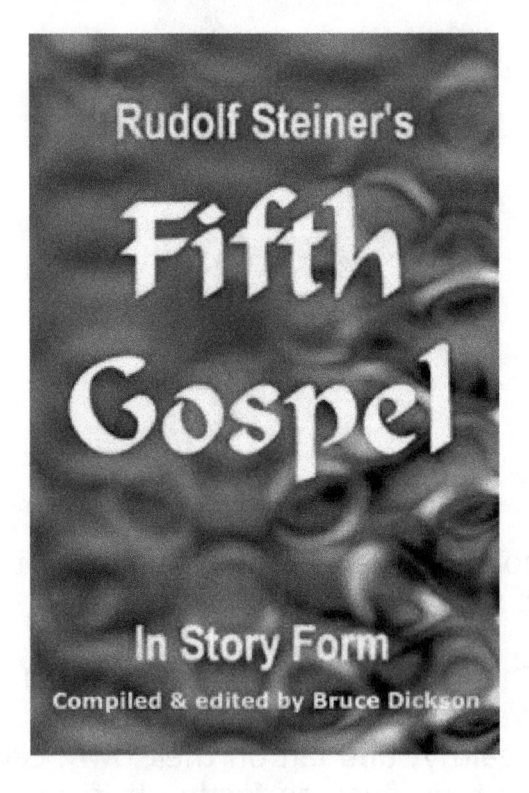

One of the wonderful experiences of my Waldorf teacher training was in a comfy living room, with a group of friends, reading aloud Rudolf Steiner's Fifth Gospel transcripts, round-robin style, a paragraph at a time. We read a chapter each night over the

HealingToolbox.org

12 Days of Christmas. If you've done this, maybe you also felt the pull to draw closer to this material. I certainly did.

Dr. Steiner's aim was to update the biography of Jesus of Nazareth, in light of the expanded psychological understanding of karma and reincarnation flourishing in the West between 1880 and 1920.

The imaginative capacity of humankind, our increased ability to process metaphor, demonstrated by Depth Psychology and Carl Jung, made possible this portrait of Jesus of Nazareth and what he transformed into. RS's Fifth Gospel remains the most psychologically astute portrait of Jesus of Nazareth this author is aware of.

An unexpected function of this material is it can support people who have lost the thread of connection with their own internal Christ spark, our immortal-eternal soul. Steiner's Fifth Gospel is an opportunity to pick up the thread of their own connection again. RS's ideas can be very healing to many conventional ideas about Jesus of Nazareth.

What Steiner found in the Akashic Records, regarding the life of Jesus of Nazareth, was a series of "story book images." These are apparently quite closely and faithfully approximated by both children's Sunday School images of the life of Christ; and also by, traditional stained glass windows of the Stations of the Cross.

If you know him, you won't be surprised to hear Steiner dove into and behind these images to

HealingToolbox.org

penetrate their inner reality; and then, articulate it in modern language for modern minds.

Steiner's verbatim lecture transcripts of his investigations were published in a book called The Fifth Gospel, but his basic clairvoyant research was never compiled nor edited; nor, was any attention paid to building a mood.

Topics include:

Inner experience of the disciples at Pentecost.

The two Jesus children, tradition of and evidence for.

Contribution of the Buddha to the Luke Jesus child.

The shepherds see the astral body of Buddha.

- How We Heal; and, Why do we get sick?

How We Heal

And, Why do we get sick?
And 35 better, more precise questions, answered by a Medical Intuitive
Bruce Dickson, MSS, MA

If I'm middle-aged or older, is it too late to change?
Why does God allow physical pain?
How come I know so little about healing myself?
Can you help me see disease from Spirit's point of view?
Where is a coherent theory of illness and wellness?
What do I have to know to heal my self?
What are trapped emotions? How do I release them?
Why won't God help me with my dis-
How do I get the attention of a Benefact
Is this a disturbance or a clearing
How much of my disease is geneti
What can illness teach us? What can I learn from
Where does disease come from?
Is examining past lives foolish escapism?
How come bad things in past lives?
Why d l it, you can heal it"?
What's the e solved childhood issues?
ing process?
I get sick?
n doctor?
How do I take b my power, ck my health from doctors?
w do Medica tuitives work
What does effective healing look ke from Spi t's point of view?
What are Best eal ng?
hat does it d?
If cells a e cons selves,
why ren t?

Including 35 better, more precise questions on wellness and healing, answered by a Medical Intuitive

Why every illness is a healing metaphor A theory of Cellular Awakening, short version.

Your personal beliefs & myths about healing.

#1: If we understand our problems, they will be healed.

HealingToolbox.org

#2: If you don't know and don't understand, then you can't heal.

#3: Personal-spiritual change takes a long time and is always a slow process. After all, you've had the problem for a long time.

#4: If you've had a negative belief for a long time, it will take a long time to change.

#5: If you change quickly, it must be superficial and not long lasting.

#6: I can't change; "This is the way I am; I'll always be this way."

#7: If you are middle-aged or older, it is too late to change.

#8: Changing old behaviors and thought patterns is often difficult and painful, "No pain, no gain."

Why is pain allowed? Why do I put up with so much pain in my body?

Can you help me see disease from Spirit's point of view?

18 more questions--answered!

Holistic Chamber Start-up Kit (2009 edition)

HealingToolbox.org

Everything you need to start your own local Holistic Chamber of Commerce .A fundraiser for local HCCs everywhere!

Each copy purchased benefits the local Chamber you buy it from. Bruce Dickson, Founder, Co-Chair ToolsThatHeal.com ~ HealingCoach.org

Camille Leon, Co-Chair ~ Westside Holistic Chamber of Commerce & http://www.holisticchamberofcommerce.com

8,000 words to inspire you to start a local chamber, where the network is, tips and hard-won experience to save you time on the front end. Concludes with some ideas you can implement once you get going.

Connect with the Author

Find Bruce at http://www.HealingToolbox.org

Gift initial sessions available for a while longer.

Bruce has a series of 15 books, 20 videos and the Inner Dashboard method.

Sessions with the author

Gift initial sessions available for a while longer. Between 8:00 am and 9:00 pm PST.

HealingToolbox@gmail.com   Skype: SelfHealingCoach

Health Intuitive Bruce Dickson shows people how to use their own Inner Dashboard so they can increase their own Inner Sunshine. How? By identifying and removing blocks and obstacles to inner Light & Sound.

With your permission, Bruce talks directly with your immune system and your own Guidance, to learn what's oppressing your cells. He shows you how to throw off burdens you no longer wish to carry.

"Working from my own limited mind is inefficient and not much fun. It works better to work from your own higher Guidance. Your Benefactors know you better than I; they know the path to your next healing better than I, so I let them lead."

Want homework? Many ways to connect with your own Guidance exist thru the Skill Ladder of Holistic Self-healing Techniques-Methods-Arts.

Let's all use more Tools That Heal and apply Best Practices in Self-Healing; including, Slow-Motion Forgiveness(SM).

Money-back guarantee on all work.

Training with the Author

If you can't go backwards

and can't remain where you are,

HealingToolbox.org

I encourage you to begin your own Heroes journey of self-healing.

If you are a holistic practitioner looking for more Tools That Heal and/or develop your own system, let's talk. Video class in the works.

Between 8:00 am and 9:00 pm PST.

HealingToolbox@gmail.com   Skype: SelfHealingCoach

Other products

Slow-Motion Forgiveness ™ Practice CD

The Five Puberties, a 3S journal on Children, 40 p. 6x9"

The Meaning of Illness Is Now an Open Book, Free 31 page PDF by request.

Muscle Testing Practice Group DVD. One hour.

1:1 phone sessions available. Group classes available. Training to do what I do is available.

Reading Group Guide for Self-healing Series

Best sellers

3) Meridian Metaphors, Psychology of the Meridians and Major Organs

11) The NEW Energy Anatomy: Nine new views of human energy; No clairvoyance required.

1) You have FIVE bodies PACME; Spiritual Geography 101. The "map" in use by all Light & Sound groups (99 cents).

2) The Meaning of Illness is Now an Open Book, Reference books to cross-reference illness and issues.

4) Your Habit Body, An Owner's Manual, the lower one-third of the "bigger you."

5) You are a Hologram Becoming Visible to Yourself

6) Self-Healing 101, Nine Experiments in Self-healing, You Can Do at Home to Awaken the Inner Healer

7) "Willingness to heal is the pre-requisite for all healing"

8) You Have Three Selves Vol. ONE; Simply the clearest model of the whole-person; Orientation

9) You Have Three Selves; Vol. TWO, Find the 3S in your life & pop culture

10) Muscle Testing as a Spiritual Exercise;

Building a Bridge to Your Body's Wisdom

12) Muscle Testing with scales of 2, 10, 100 & 1000

Measuring invisible energies with 'God as your Partner'

More advanced titles

13) The Inner Court: Close-up of the Habit Body

14) The Five Puberties, Growing new eyes to see children and maturation afresh.

15) Radical Cell Wellness—Especially for women!

Books outside the Best Practices Series

Rudolf Steiner's Fifth Gospel in Story Form

Stand-alone 99 cent eBooks tangential to Best Practices Series

From Five Animal Senses to 12 or More Human Senses

Forgive from Your Soul, Slow Motion Forgiveness, the Missing Manual

How We Heal; and, Why do we get sick? Including 35 more precise Q&A on wellness.

HealingToolbox.org

Other CLASSICS of self-healing & Medical Intuition

MSIA Discourses http://www.msia.org/discourses

Forgiveness, Key to the Kingdom, John-Roger

The Emotion Code, Bradley Nelson

Messages From the Body, Michael Lincoln

Our Many Selves, Elizabeth O'Connor

Touch for Health, 2nd Ed, Mathew Thie

Your Body Speaks Your Mind, 2nd ed. Deb Shapiro

Core Transformation, Connierae Andreas

The best solution is always loving

Did you enjoy this? Please share.

If you get stuck, give me a call.

HealingToolbox.org